MW00426411

The Truth I Believe

Devotions for Women

By Tiffany Thibault

Deuteronomy 6:7 - You shall teach them diligently to your children, and shall talk of them when you sit in your house, and when you walk by the way, and when you lie down, and when you rise.

I am thankful for the spiritual legacy that runs through my family tree. I dedicate this book to those who came before me, who faithfully walked with the Lord; and to my precious daughters, whose stories fill these pages. I pray that you always treasure the things of God that you have been taught through the years as we sat together, walked together and prayed together. I pray for you as you continue on your own personal faith journey of loving Jesus more and more each new day.

Table of Contents

Lemons or Limes?

Psalm 103:2-5 - Bless the LORD, O my soul, and forget not all His benefits, who forgives all your iniquity, who heals all your disease, who redeems your life from the pit, who crowns you with steadfast love and mercy, who satisfies you with good so that your youth is renewed like eagles.

I was born a blonde. Over the years as my natural hair darkened, I kept it blonde with hair dye. When I was younger, I joked about my forgetfulness, blaming it on being blonde (sorry other blondes). When I turned thirty, then forty, I blamed my forgetfulness on my age. Regardless of what I blamed it on, it didn't change the fact that I forget things often in the busyness of my days.

It happened once again this past spring. I was at Costco with my daughter and we saw some dwarf citrus trees. I had the perfect pot waiting for one, so I bought the one with the tiniest white flower buds, lugged it home and planted it, throwing away the information tag that came with the tree.

I enjoyed watching the flowers turn into tiny little fruit balls and over the summer I loved seeing the green fruit growing larger. Somewhere over the months I forgot what type of tree I had planted. I thought it was a lime tree, but my daughter was convinced it was a lemon.

One day I was making some guacamole and went out to my patio and picked two perfect "limes" from my tree. I sliced them in half and squeezed the juice into the bowl. It was tart and perfect! My daughter became annoyed that I had harvested some fruit and said to me, "Mom those are lemons, you just have to wait and trust me. I remember what kind we bought!"

I decided to wait and see who was right. Days and weeks passed. Those small perfect round limes, well they began to grow larger, stretch into a different shape, and are now turning yellow. It is definitely a lemon tree. My daughter's memory is correct. We are now currently waiting to harvest about eleven lemons. I know I will never forget what type of tree this is in the years to come because I have had personal experience in seeing it grow and change.

The Psalmist in our verse, is telling his soul to:

"Bless the Lord, and do not forget the amazing things that God has done for him."

Why? Because in our human brokenness, and our life of busyness, we so quickly forget who the LORD is and what amazing things He has done in our life already. We forget that He has forgiven us, healed us, redeemed us, crowned us! I forgot what type of tree I had, but because I now SEE the truth, I will never forget.

So how do we move from reading these words in the Bible, to never forgetting the goodness of God? Well, we have the information in front of us (the Bible) to remind us. We have to purposefully move the words from the pages to our soul, before we can own them, before we can truly believe them. We do that by speaking its truth so often that we begin to believe it, and when that happens, we can then live it. Write it down, listen to it, read it out loud, fill your space with God's word. The more we hear it, the more bits of it will sink deep into our soul. Remind yourselves and do it often, of what things God has already done in your soul and life.

When we remind ourselves of the truth, we can never forget.

As my daughter and I await the lemons fully ripening, we are dreaming of lemon bars, lemon meringue pie, and sweet lemonade. All these thoughts solidify in my tired brain EXACTLY what type of fruit it is and I know I will NEVER forget this fact ever.

As you wait for God to work in your circumstances, remind yourself of His work in the past and wait with excitement, His continued work in your life. He is worthy of your praise today and tomorrow. He is worthy of your remembering His work in your past. He is worthy of your trusting Him for how He will most definitely work in your days to come. Bless Him, and don't ever forget Him. The work He is doing will indeed be a sweet fruit in your life.

First published March 19, 2020 at www.ibelieve.com

Seeking God with All Our Hearts

Jeremiah 29:13 - You will seek me and find me when you seek me with all your heart.

I love Spring and I love Easter. I get excited when those little plastic eggs hit the store shelves. I get them early and fill them with jelly beans and chocolate eggs. I love it so much that I tend to stuff a generous number of eggs, even though we usually only have two children hunting for them!

On Easter morning, my husband slips outside to hide the eggs. He places them in easy to locate spots, but also in spots that the kids may not ever notice, or simply walk right by without even seeing them.

When he is finished hiding the eggs, the girls grab their baskets and quickly run around outside, checking under bushes and up into the tree branches. Those little eggs can be found snuggled into a leafy bush, resting inside a flower, and laying on the window ledge. Some eggs have found themselves on top of the bird feeder, on the pool waterfall, and under the doormat.

After the hunt is over, the girls empty their candy into their basket and then hide the eggs again for each other to find, just for fun.

I love the words of this Bible verse:

*"You will seek me and find me
when you seek me with all your heart."*

The Lord has done so much for us! The Easter season is a celebration of how He died and rose again for us, so that we can have NEW life. He gives us the promise that if we seek Him with all our hearts, we *will* find Him.

My girls don't casually hunt for their eggs. No, they usually are running to find them. My sweet girls who usually share well, turn into super competitive egg hunters. For them, it's an 'each man for himself' kind of mentality. Nothing deters them from seeking for eggs with every single part of their being. Their satisfaction is in having a filled basket.

What if we were to seek the Lord with that type of dogged determination? What if nothing could hold us back? Our verse promises us that we will find God if we seek Him.

My girls prepare for their hunt by not only seeing their Easter baskets sitting on the table for days, but talking about it as they wait in anticipation for the hunt. My girls never give up seeking for eggs after finding just a few. They continue to seek.

Can you join me in seeking the Lord in as many moments each day as possible?

Seeking God is as easy as learning to pray in every situation (good or bad) and asking God for wisdom as you walk through it.

Seeking God starts as we open the Bible each day, praying for Him to reveal Himself through the words. We can cling to the promise our verse gives that we will find Him!

Let's make this season a new start for us spiritually. Together, let's pray words of thankfulness, read His words and seek Him with everything we have! Let's dust off our Bibles and open them. Let's eagerly seek Him today and tomorrow, until we know Him more than we ever thought we could!

First published April 9, 2020 at www.ibelieve.com

How to Flourish in Hard Times

Proverbs 17:1 - Better a dry crust with peace and quiet than a house full of feasting, with strife.

Tough times definitely bring out the insecurities and the weaknesses of a person's character. Turn on any crime TV show and you will see what happens when people let their emotions control them. So how do we get through these times with peace and quiet, as our verse says? Let me share with you an experience from my childhood.

My family struggled financially for some of my growing up years. My dad struggled for several years to find a job, sometimes even hiring on daily as a construction worker. We actually lived in other people's homes for six months, as my parents couldn't make the rent payment. Our only car was repossessed. At one point we only ate two meals a day, for many months, and my parents relied on food banks to help us get by.

I remember one cold winter while living in Colorado. The power was turned off for a few days and we had to take cold showers and wash our clothes in the bathtub. It was around this time that my 16-year-old brother started working at Arby's to help, while I cleaned a few houses and babysat to help out as well (at the age of 15).

It was difficult. My parents were stressed for sure but turned to the Lord often in prayer. Financial struggles are really, really hard. Fear is the enemy in a time like this. We worry about how to make ends meet, and where we can find any extra money to make those ends meet.

Today, news reports are predicting a tough economic future ahead. Many of us are looking at cutbacks at work, or even losing our jobs due to the sudden, drastic change. Fear tries to grip our hearts as we worry about paying bills.

One thing though, through this all, we still have our families, our friend, our church communities and our neighbors. We have one another, always.

Our Bible verse says:

"Better a dry crust with peace and quiet than a house full of feasting, with strife."

During this tough time, let's take this opportunity to build strong marriages and strong families.

This situation is not your husband's, wife's or even kid's fault. It happened.

Here are two basic principles to guide your days:

1. We must get more intentional about prayer and reading God's word.

We can start by being intentional about increasing our prayers and strengthening our faith, as we fill ourselves with the promises from the Bible. Can you take time throughout your day to read the Bible or even just one verse? Can you practice being quick to pray as each new situation comes your way?

As we allow God to fill us with Him, we can reflect peace and quiet to those under our roof. We can trust Him to get us through. We will then have peace and can react calmly to our family. Let's moment by moment place our fears into the hands of God.

2. We should make it a priority and value to find and create moments of joy each day.

Another easy thing to do is to be intentional about creating moments of joy in our homes for our family.

When my family was struggling, my mom created joy by having a movie or game night every single night.

We may not have had snacks, but my parents intentionally created some moments of fun. It was critical to our survival as a family.

When I look back on my childhood, I remember those movie nights, as we all squeezed onto the sofa. I remember taking walks in the falling snow late one night, just because. I remember my mom breaking out in silly singing. I remember her reading us promises from scripture and discussing it over our two meals each day. I remember her having each of us kids plan and lead devotions for the family.

God did get my family through that situation. He will also get your family through this time as well. He has a plan at work in your life, for your today and all your tomorrows.

Someday, let's look back and see that God blessed us during hard times with strong families and strong communities.

What good is plenty, when relationships are at strife? I would give up all feasting and be happy with only a dry crust of bread to eat, if it meant my husband and I lived in peace and quiet together. Let's reach out to our spouses and be intentional about living in harmony through this difficult situation. My family is worth it. Your family is worth it.

First published April 17, 2020 at www.ibelieve.com

How Love Covers a Multitude of Sins

1 Peter 1:48 - Above all, love each other deeply, because love covers over a multitude of sins.

It's easy to love the lovable, to love the ones who make your life easier, to love the ones who add value to your life. It's downright near impossible to love the ones who bring you pain, especially when it's intentionally done.

According to our verse here in 1 Peter, we who say that we are Christians, need to work at making it a priority to show love to others, even to those who cause pain, for we are not perfect. We are not without sin. We ourselves desperately need the love of a Savior.

The words tell us to:

"love each other deeply"

This means that we are quick to forgive, that we work to overlook past hurts that others have done to us, and that we encourage others who are struggling.

It does not mean that we stay in an unsafe situation, bringing even more pain. It might even mean protecting our hearts as we strive to forgive, working to move beyond the pain. It might even mean to walk away from people, even relatives, who cause you continual pain.

When my daughter was about three, we had a large yellow lab named Buddy. He absolutely adored my daughter!

One day as she and I took Buddy for his afternoon walk, she wanted to hold his leash as he strolled beside us on the sidewalk.

She had been walking him at her pace for some time, when all of a sudden, a rabbit darted past him. Buddy took off in wild pursuit, dragging my poor daughter across the grass behind him. I yelled at her to let go of the leash as I lunged at him to catch him.

My daughter sat up, then looked down at her scraped-up knees and began to sob hysterically at the smarting pain.

I carried her home, holding firmly to the dog's leash.

Once home, after her little knees had been cleaned and covered with princess bandages, she called Buddy over to her.

She gave him a big hug and said, "Buddy, I love you and I forgive you."

When her dad came home from work a few days later, her scrapes were completely healed. She told her daddy what had happened and said, "Buddy didn't mean to hurt me, but I forgave him anyway."

I have often thought about her pure truth and simplicity in this situation. She had been hurt, but it didn't stop her from quickly forgiving. She didn't hold it against Buddy and withhold her love. He didn't understand what forgiveness meant, but she did need to let him know that he was forgiven. It was necessary for her healing.

As I look at circumstances I am walking through, I find myself examining how quick I am to forgive someone for the cruel things that they say or do.

When I fail to forgive quickly, I do find that it becomes easy to nurse my hurt, to fuel the pain. My resistance to loving that person by holding onto my hurt, in actuality really only hurts me. They have probably moved on from what they said or did, if they even remember it at all!

I am not showing love to myself or to them if I cannot love them. I cannot love them as Christ desires if I am harboring unforgiveness or anger toward them.

I alone hold the power to forgive them, and thus show the love of Christ. This doesn't mean that I need to ever see that person again, it just means that I am relinquishing any power they might have over my heart.

Ephesians 4:26 says:

"Do not let the sun go down on your anger."

The longer we allow the pain, the anger to linger, the better chance it has of taking root, and preventing love to flourish. If we can practice quickly forgiving, we can prevent bitterness from taking root.

As you read these words today, whose name comes to mind?

I want to challenge you today to find a way to forgive that person who has said or done things to hurt you. It isn't easy on our own, but we do have the Lord on our side.

Matthew 19:26 says this:

"With Him all things are possible!"

I must state here, that what I am writing about is purposefully forgiving comments and situations as they unintentionally arise.

If you are dealing with painful past hurts or relationship issues that are overwhelming you or endangering you, please seek professional help or counseling to walk beside you, as you find the strength to be able to forgive those people, to find healing, and to be freed from the burden of the pain they caused.

First published May 29, 2020 at www.crosswalk.com

Surprise Others with Love

John 13:35 - By this all men will know that you are my disciples, if you love one another.

It was one of those mornings. I did my best to rush through getting ready, to run out the door to try to get to my college class on time. I threw my book bag on the passenger seat, then started my car. The gas indicator was in the red "E" zone! My brother had borrowed my car for work the night before, and had not replaced the gas he had used. I knew that I didn't have time to stop at the gas station without being late. I could only hope I could get to the college with the gas that was left in the tank.

I tensely drove down the interstate, praying that I could make it to college without running out of gas. I *almost* made it. I put on my indicator to take my exit, when the car sputtered and began to slow. I pulled over to the side of the road and turned the car off. I was one mile from the college.

I grabbed my purse, and began to walk along the side of the interstate, planning to walk to the nearest gas station and get a can of gas.

As I walked, fuming at the situation, I heard a car slowly pull up behind me. I heard a voice call out, "Can I give you a ride?" I turned to see a young woman about my age, poking her head out the window. She said she had seen me walking as she drove down the opposite side of the interstate. She had taken the next exit and came back to help me.

She said "We girls need to help each other!"

I jumped in her car, then she drove me to the gas station and waited as I paid for a can of gas, then drove me back to my car. I thanked the lady for her help and worried that she would be late to work. She waved her hand and said not to worry about it, that she was glad she was at the right place and time to help me.

I never saw that lady again.

I never let my car get below ¼ tank of gas again and I made my brother replace any gas he used.

More than that though, I am still blessed that a total stranger went out of her way to help me by looking after my interests above her own. She wanted to make sure that I wasn't picked up or harassed by someone meaning me harm. She knew I was capable of walking to the gas station by myself. She knew she was on her way to work, and would probably be late herself. Instead, she chose to help me.

In preschool a common phrase we teach kids is to "be kind" and "to share". We want to teach kids empathy, the ability to think about other people's needs. We adults are not exempt from being kind.

Jesus taught His disciples this when He told them to:

"Do to others as you would have them do to you." (Luke 6:31)

He saw their humanness, their self-centeredness coming out. Jesus also said:

"By this all men will know that you are my disciples, if you love one another." (John 13:35)

It has become so normal in our culture to determine that our needs are the most important ones, without thinking about anyone else. Jesus says that our love will show the world who we serve, so are we truly living this out?

I love to see the absolute surprise on people's faces when I put their needs before my own. Niceness shouldn't ever be a surprise to people. Let's make it the norm. Will you make it your goal to "love surprise" people today? Here are a few quick ways to "love surprise people":

> Allow someone to go in front of you at the store because they have less to buy than you.

Take someone's shopping cart back to the store for them.

Smile at a stranger who looks down and give them an encouraging word.

Give the mail delivery person a cold bottle of water on a hot day.

Buy a homeless person a meal.

Send a little note or email of encouragement to someone, thanking them for who or what they are.

At the end of the day, can you look back and see where you showed the world *whose* disciple you are, by serving others in love? Let's impact the world together, you and I, as we "love surprise" those people whom God has put in our path.

First published June 10, 2020 at www.crosswalk.com

The Journey Through Grief

Psalm 34:18 - The Lord is close to the broken hearted; He rescues those whose spirits are crushed.

Grief is nobody's friend, yet to each one of us, it will come knocking at our doors. We suddenly become acquainted with its constant presence, until we can relearn to laugh again, until the pain becomes tolerable. This lesson of walking through grief cannot be taught, it has to be learned through experience.

When a loved one dies, their passing is cleanly tied up with a service and a burial. Grief though, is not clean and it is not pretty. Ever.

I have walked through the passage of grief over the past few years.

I have come to the place of smiling again, of laughing, of dreaming.

However, there are moments that still wash over me with a powerful wave of intense sorrow that randomly comes out of nowhere, when I least expect it, leaving me in the throes of fresh grief.

Those moments usually come as a result of someone else's unintentional casual words that scrape the surface of my heart.

You see, I grieve for my lost child, for the loss of a lifetime of firsts, for the lifetime of dreams I wanted for that child.

I never got to hold my son, who never opened his eyes, who never cried his first cry, and whose fingers and toes were still being formed. Just because he never fully grew does not mean that my grief was any less real or valid. Grief doesn't pass out lesser sentences because someone wasn't "as old" as someone else.

The casual comments from people about "well, it's for the best" and "it's God's will" never help one recover from grief any sooner.

Another well-meaning comment of "you weren't that far along" didn't make the grief any less easy to carry. Even the words: "be glad you just have two kids" can slam me with the heartbroken reminder that my days will never be filled with the voice of the child I was never able to raise.

In those initial weeks of grief, when I felt like hiding away from the "well meaning" comments of other Christians, I clung to this Bible verse in Psalm 34:18:

> *"The Lord is close to the brokenhearted; He rescues those whose spirits are crushed."*

We can find two promises in this verse:

1. *The Lord is close to the brokenhearted.*

He sees our heart. He sees that it is broken. He also saw His child die. When Jesus walked on the earth, He wept for the death of His dear friend, whom He then raised back to life again. He had to grieve for him, before He could see new life.

As you walk through the things that break your heart, know that the Lord is near. He longs to be your comfort. It was during my dark days of grief that I found solace in reading the book of Psalms. Those writers poured out all their emotions before the Lord.

2. *He rescues those whose spirits are crushed.*

As we are able to keep seeking the Lord and keep pouring our hearts out to Him, He will rescue us someday. He will take those crushed spirits and He will restore and renew. It will be in His timing. It can't be rushed, and it won't always be in the way that we think we want.

If you know a parent who has lost their child before it was time to be born, love on them. Don't offer those "well-meaning words" that don't make any sense to the one who grieves. They are mourning. Allow them to grieve. Let them mourn for as long as they need to.

During my time of grief, there was a friend who let me cry and who truly understood for she had walked the same path. Her gentleness was evident. It was healing. It was the life ring I needed to keep from drowning.

You could also give the parent something tangible. My sister-in-law mailed me a cross with a sweet message on the back about my son. Each year I shed a tear as I hang it with my other children's ornaments on my Christmas tree. Her recognizing my son's life, though it was indeed brief, was the most incredible healing part of my journey.

There will come a day when all who grieve *will be able* to laugh, to continue on their journey. Maybe the purpose in the pain is so that we can be the hands and feet of the Lord.

Can you set aside your thoughts and opinions and just show love to the grieving, to point them to the Lord? A hug and a listening ear are more valuable than anything else. Let the Lord speak to their heart through your love.

Our loved one's will never completely leave us, but we will continue to find a way to put one step forward continuing on our journey.

We cling to the Lord and to the promise of seeing our loved ones in Heaven. Our time on earth is indeed short, but we look forward to an eternity with them at our side as we worship our God together.

First published July 7, 2020 at www.ibelieve.com

The Blessings of Obedience

Deuteronomy 28:1 - If you fully obey the Lord your God and carefully follow all His commands I give you today, the Lord your God will set you high above all the nations on earth.

My husband decided to get a puppy for the family. He was super little and super cute. However, he was not housebroken and had no clue of what the house rules were. He had accidents everywhere. He knocked over his water bowl. He spilled his food. He cried all through his first night with us and no one got any sleep.

We quickly discovered that Oscar was extremely stubborn. He wanted to do things his way, all the time. He was also growing bigger and bolder every day. He nipped at the kids, he tore apart my daughter's stuffed animals and he growled at me. Walking him was no fun as he would try to pull ahead.

He barked every single night for absolutely no reason, except to keep me awake (because it seemed that I was the only one who heard him!) Something had to be done, and soon.

So, we hired a trainer for some one-on-one training. He taught us how to get Oscar to respect us. Finally, Oscar obeyed us during the day, walks became more enjoyable, and a white noise fan helped him (and me) to sleep through the night.

Oscar has been with us now for five years. He is still stubborn, but he has realized we are the boss. Oscars' respect for us came from his understanding that he had to fully obey. Our rules are not only to keep him safe, but also to allow us to enjoy him more.

How do you view God? Do you view the things He asks us to do in the Bible as optional? Do you pick and choose what you feel comfortable obeying?

As Christians, in our struggles of living in this world, we often find ourselves at a crossroads of having to choose between living according to the standards of our culture, or living it according to the way that the Bible lays out how we should live. Sometimes the decision is easy, other times it is not.

Choosing to follow God's rules can at times be very hard. It can make us feel different. It can cause rejection from others.

But what if we were to see God's commands as a way to receive His blessings, instead of seeing His law as a joy killer or as punishment?

There are two Bible verses which stand out in my mind regarding the reward of obeying God's commands.

First is Deuteronomy 28:1:

"If you fully obey the Lord your God and carefully follow all His commands I give you today, the Lord your God will set you high above all the nations on earth."

Also, this verse from Deuteronomy 5:33:

"Walk in obedience to all that the Lord your God has commanded you, so that you may live and prosper and prolong your days in the land that you will possess."

I love to walk my dog when he is being obedient. I am happy and want to give him treats and praise for how he obeys. However, when he is being super stubborn and refusing to listen to me, I cannot end the walk soon enough and I do not reward him with praise or treats, because well, he didn't choose to obey me.

God gives you a choice every single day and in every situation.

He wants you to fully obey Him out of your love for Him.

He gives you amazing promises of blessings when you chose to obey Him.

Why not today, as you walk with the Lord, you look for opportunities to obey Him and see if He will not send blessings upon your life?

First published August 10, 2020 at www.ibelieve.com

Is Your Light Shining Before Others?

Matthew 5:16 - Let your light so shine before men, that they may see your good works and glorify your Father in heaven.

When I was setting up my baby's nursery, I made sure that there was a night light in the room. I knew that I would be very grateful for the low light it gave so that I would not stumble in the dark as I cared for my newborn in the middle of the night.

As my children grew and moved out of their cribs, into big girl beds, and then into their separate bedrooms, they always wanted to have a night light on. One little light shone in the bathroom, and one was turned on by their beds. When they determined that they were too old for a baby night light, they still wanted me to keep the hall light on for them until they fell asleep.

Those lights I left on kept the scary things away. It was bright enough to illuminate the good and familiar things in their room. It brought peace to them. It dispelled the scary thoughts. It allowed them to fall asleep without fear.

We are living in such an amazing time. At the click of a button, we can have access to instant information, both good and bad. Unfortunately, it often seems that the bad outweighs the good. Relationships are hurting. Hearts are hopeless. Lives are riddled with fear and anxiety.

Our Bible verse tells us to:

*"Let our light shine so that people
can see our good works
and when they do,
they will praise our Father in heaven."*

In our world of fear, bad news, scary moments, and uncertainty, this is the very time that we need to turn our lights on. We need to make sure that we are plugged into the Word, are spending time studying the Bible and praying, for its then that God will shine through us. The more we plug into Jesus, the more we will crave reflecting His love and peace to others.

This is pointed out to us in Colossians 3:16-17:

*"Let the message of Christ
dwell among you richly
as you teach and admonish one another
with all wisdom through
psalms, hymns, and songs from the Spirit,
singing to God with gratitude in your hearts.
And whatever you do, whether in word or deed,
do it all in the name of the Lord Jesus, giving
thanks to God the Father through Him."*

Just as I was happy to leave the light on for my small children, as it was comforting to them, those living in the world around us desperately need the light. They desperately need hope as well. Darkness brings shadows that imaginations can make into terrifying shapes and situations. The light always brings illumination. People need to see that there is hope, that there is another way to walk through their days.

Jesus says that:

"We are the light of the world –
like a city on a hilltop that cannot be hidden.
No one lights a lamp
and then puts it under a basket.
Instead, a lamp is placed on a stand,
where it gives light to everyone in the house."
(Matthew 5:14-15)

How bright is your light shining? Are you hiding the reason for your hope under a basket, or under the bottom of your priorities?

To turn the night light on for my girls required action on my part. We need to have action if we are going to reflect the light of Jesus.

What are you doing intentionally this year to fill yourself with the light of Jesus?

This year I am being super intentional about my daily quiet time reading the Word. I know how vital it is, but I also know how weak I am sticking with it.

So, this year I recruited my teenage daughters to read a Bible plan with me on an app. Their accountability is working!

Can you find someone today to help you be accountable for your quiet time? Let's not put off one more day of growing closer to Jesus. Open His Word and let His love flow through you today.

First published August 13, 2020 at www.ibelieve.com

Are You in a Desert Season?

Hosea 13:5 - I cared for you in the wilderness, in the land of drought.

I have lived in the desert off and on for many years. I have learned that life in the desert offers some guarantees. Summers will be VERY hot. Dust will become a constant battle. My skin will be dry and my car battery will need to be replaced every 3-ish years. Desert life is hard on everyone and everything.

For many years I lived on the edge of the city; my neighborhood edged by a nature preserve for desert tortoises. Walking trails abounded back in this desert area. In the winter months I would take my dog for walks out there. I rarely saw another person. I loved the solitude, the quiet from the hectic city down the hill. I loved to watch the desert go through its winter and spring season.

But by the time the temps warmed up it became unbearable to walk out there, with the days warming into the triple digits.

Through the long summer months, I impatiently waited for the temperatures to cool so I could once again walk in the wilderness.

On many of my walks on the trails through the cactus and shrub brush, though the places seemed uninhabitable, there were tiny signs of life. Occasionally I would see rabbits, chipmunks, lizards, and birds. I walked with care, as I also knew that rattlesnakes lived out there. At night we sometimes even heard coyotes howling or saw bats swooping around.

As I lived my days in the desert, I would often think about the Israelites and their journey through the wilderness. In our lives of walking with the Lord, we too sometimes feel as though we are walking through wilderness.

There will be times when it's hard to read the Bible, to trust that God truly means what He says. There will be times when we long for rain, for something to quench our spiritual thirst.

The Israelites left Egypt, the land where they had lived as slaves for many, many years. In delivering them from slavery, God led them to the wilderness and had them wander around there for 40 years. The days were long, the summers hot, the winters cold. They complained and longed for the sweet fruit and meat that they remembered from Egypt.

It was there in the wilderness though, that God provided for them. Every single day, He delivered fresh food. He guided them as to where to go next and He protected them. It was there in the desert that they received their first written word from God.

They often focused on the dirt, the heat, the cold, the inconveniences of living the hard life that wilderness living brings, and when they took their eyes off of God and focused on their woes, life grew even harder, and God seemed more distant.

Similarly, when we are going through really hard times, it seems like we are all alone, struggling through the difficulties. It feels as though God is not even there, or that He doesn't even care.

It is during the times of walking through the wilderness that we must recognize that God is caring for us. He says this in Hosea:

> *"I cared for you in the wilderness,
> in the land of drought."* (Hosea 13:5)

In the midst of our lack or our discomfort during those times, we must intentionally look for the ways He is caring for us through it.

We must recognize that the wilderness is imperative for our faith, our reliance upon God.

Jesus knew how hard we struggle and He gave us this promise:

*"Come to me, all you who are weary and
burdened, and I will give you rest.
Take my yoke upon you and learn from me,
for I am gentle and humble in heart,
and you will find rest for your souls.
For my yoke is easy and my burden is light."*
(Matthew 11:28-30)

The lessons that we learn in the wilderness are the very ones that God will use to grow our faith, give power to our testimony, and draw us closer to Him.

If we lived every day in a beautiful greenhouse, we would never learn to be strong against the heat, the storms, or the attack of pests. Our faith is like this.

We need to be thirsty enough to need the refreshing of God's word.

We need to be hungry enough to desire God's word.

We need to be tired enough of our wandering, to get back on track with the Lord.

Once the Israelites had learned the lessons that God had for them, they were then strong enough to enter the Promised Land. The things they learned equipped them to go and do battle to take the land for their families.

So, if you are wandering in the wilderness right now, let the promise of this verse encourage you:

> *"So, let's not get tired of doing what is good. At just the right time we will reap a harvest of blessing if we don't give up."* (Galatians 6:9)

Remember that God is caring for you through every single moment of this journey.

First published September 9, 2020 at www.ibelieve.com

Do Not Forget What You Have Seen

Deuteronomy 4:9 - Only give heed to yourself and keep your soul diligently, so that you do not forget the things which your eyes have seen and they do not depart from your heart all the days of your life; but make them known to your sons and your grandsons.

My little girl was about 3 ½ when she cheerfully volunteered to go get the mail. She had been doing this for a few days now. Our mailbox was at the curb of our driveway, part of a quiet cul-de-sac. The first day or two that she got the mail, I stood at the door and watched her.

Today though, she said, "Mama, I'm a big girl. I can get the mail. Don't watch me."

I said ok, and let her go to get the mail without watching her.

I instead, went into the kitchen to start making lunch, telling myself that independence has to come in baby steps such as this.

She skipped down the driveway, proud of being a big girl.

She opened the door of the mailbox and grabbed the mail out. Then she saw a piece of paper in the newspaper slot. She reached her sweet little hand into the slot to get the paper. Then she began to scream at the top of her lungs.

When I heard that little girl scream, I ran to the front door, threw it open and ran outside, seeing my daughter crying and hearing her blood curdling screams.

When my daughter had reached her hand into the newspaper slot, she had not noticed the wasp nest. She had been stung by a wasp. The surprise and pain caused her to scream in hurt and anger.

When I reached her and said, "Honey what happened?"

She said, "A bad bee mama, a bad bee hurt me!"

I saw her little red and swollen finger. I picked her up and carried her in the house, using soothing tones to calm her down.

I cleaned the finger, wrapped it in a Band-Aid and then we snuggled on the sofa, talking about her scary moment. Hugs, kisses and little Band-Aids go a very long way in healing a hurt finger.

Though this happened about 13 years ago, my daughter still remembers the shock of that wasp sting. She didn't stop going to get the mail every day for me, but she did add a new habit to her routine. From that point on, she squatted and looked into the newspaper slot before reaching her hand in. When her little sister got old enough to look into the mailbox, my daughter got her in the habit of always looking first, always looking for wasps.

Our Bible verse tells us to focus on our self and to examine our soul diligently.

We are the ones who are responsible to be sure that we remember the things we have seen, the ways that God has used our pain, the way that God has worked through our struggles.

We are the ones who see that God has moved when it seemed impossible.

We are the only ones responsible for our spiritual life, our relationship with God. We must be so careful about not only guarding it, but also cultivating it.

Jesus told his disciples:

"To watch and pray." (Luke 21:36)

Jesus knows how easily we can forget the truths of God. We are to walk with the Lord, clinging to His promises. We are to teach the truth to our children and our grandchildren.

Related, I love to hear of someone using their grandma's recipe. Why? Because something good is being shared with the next generation. Our faith should be just as sweet as grandma's cookie recipe, it should be so important to us, that we diligently protect it, grow it and share it with the next generation.

Neither of my daughters have been stung by a wasp again. They have remembered to look diligently before reaching out. Our faith and our history of trust in God should also protect us from foolishly, blindly repeating the same reason for the pain.

Today, will you trust Him a little more, seek Him a little more and share Him a little more than you have ever done before?

Will you join me in seeing that our relationship with the Lord is actively growing as seek Him through His word each and every day?

First published September 17, 2020 at www.ibelieve.com

You Are a Light in the Dark World

John 1:4-5 - In Him was life, and that life was the light of all mankind. The light shines in the darkness, and the darkness has not overcome it.

I love to go to the theatre. Once I have purchased my tickets, I impatiently wait for the night of the event. I love to arrive early and to be handed a playbill on the way to my seat. I find it fascinating to read the bios about the actors and actresses. Having a little bit of insight into who the actors are in their real world adds so much to the roles that they act out before me in the theater world.

Excitement builds in me as the lights begin their warning flicker to hurry latecomers to their seats.

The lights over the audience dims into darkness as the lights above the stage turn on and the curtain opens to reveal the stage set to tell a story.

The next few hours as the story unfolds, the actors and actresses are illuminated as the audience sits in darkness.

The focus is on the stage and the scene that is playing out before you. Even though the light is not shining on the dark audience, there is enough light from the stage to allow any audience member to safely exit their seat to leave the theatre, without needing any other light. The dark theatre is not too dark to overcome the light on the stage.

Now let's think about our daily life. We are also on stage, playing the various parts that have emerged and developed in our own lives. We hold roles such as wives, mothers, daughters, workers, chefs, volunteer, and the list goes on. Though we have many roles, one thing is constant: our faith stays with us in each situation.

Jesus told a parable about hiding our faith from the world and compared it to putting a lamp under a bowl.

Matthew 5:15 says this:

"Neither do people light a lamp and
put it under a bowl.
Instead, they put it on a stand.
Then it gives light to everyone in the house."

How silly it would be if I were to invite people over for a dinner party and turn on a lamp and put it in the closet. It would do no good to anyone at that party. We wouldn't be able to see what we were eating, or where we were walking. The entire party would be a waste of time and effort.

We live in a world full of people stumbling in the dark. They do not know God. Many of them though, do know that we know God. They are definitely watching our actions and listening to our words.

If we are walking close to the Lord and filling ourselves with more of Him through studying our Bibles, then His light and love should radiate from us. The way we are speaking and acting (behaving) in our lives, should be shining brightly to those who are lost, broken, and stumbling in the darkness of their depression, their pain, or their wandering.

As you go through your day, can you think of any times when you can shine a little brighter for Jesus?

Who is in your path that you can cast some Jesus into their darkness?

People everywhere need hope, they need a smile, they need to know that they truly matter.

Let's determine together to allow Jesus to shine through us, to not stop from speaking His truth when someone is crying out from the darkness.

Perhaps you are the only one that can help that one person who crosses your path today. Let Jesus shine through you today.

First published September 29, 2020 at www.ibelieve.com

How Sin Sticks to Us

The other day I was sitting in the dentist chair for my bi-annual checkup. As the hygienist was carefully chipping away at the tartar buildup on my one stubborn tooth, I began to think about how tartar and sin are similar. We eat whole foods, we floss, brush and rinse well, but some of that tartar finds a way to hold on and stick so tightly that only an expert can remove it.

In the same way, sin has a way of sneaking into our lives, sticking to us, building up to such an extent that it actually becomes a part of us. It becomes our norm. We get so used to it being there that we forget all about it. We become super comfortable with it as it settles into place.

We are super good at lying to others and ourselves in our feeble attempts to cover up our sin.

But God, He is not content for that sin to remain in our lives. He sends people and circumstances our way to stretch us, to stress us, to illuminate

---

the areas of sin that have become comfortable to us.

These people and circumstances can shake us up so much that we can clearly see the areas of sin sticking to our lives.

It would be a poor hygienist indeed if she were to send me home without adequately cleaning my teeth. In our hearts, as the Lord reveals the areas of hidden sin in our lives, we must remove it.

James 4:17 says this:

> *"So, whoever knows the right thing to do and fails to do it, for him it is sin."*

Just as we should be intentional about dental care between our dental visits, we need to be intentional about examining our hearts, our actions and our attitudes for places where sin might be sneaking in.

Our verse from Acts 3:19 says that this is an action that depends on me intentionally changing my heart and my life, and turning back to God, only then will my sins be wiped away.

I know that when I became a believer my sins were forgiven, but I am also very aware that while I live in my human body that it is super easy to slip into sin.

Attitudes become thoughts that become comfortable sin patterns. It's like if SIN came through my door, put on my slippers, took a snack from the refrigerator, got comfy on my sofa and is planning to hang out for the weekend. It's like a guest that will never leave unless I kick him to the curb.

I pray that we all will examine our hearts and see the areas where sin is hiding. Let's quickly kick it from our lives, so that we can be free of it, for only then will we see a change in our hearts and lives as we determine to keep living for Jesus.

First published October 5, 2020 at www.ibelieve.com

When God Looks Down from Heaven

Psalm 53:2 - God looks down from heaven on all mankind to see if there are any who understand, any who seek God.

When you are flying high up in the sky and look out the window to the earth below, this is what you can see: the rivers look like sparkling ribbons, curving and twisting down the back of a girl's long hair. The tiny houses and yards look like homes where Tinkerbell could live. The farm fields are filled with crops varying in their colors, like patchwork on a beautiful quilt. The tiny boats are bobbing on the water, clearly pointing out the massiveness of our oceans.

This is why I love to have the window seat when I am flying on a plane. I love to look down at my hometown as we take off and the new city as we land. Everything looks different when seen from above. I see things as I look down that are not so clear when I am on the ground looking around me. Buildings look shorter, homes seem smaller, rivers seem longer, deserts seem more desolate, and mountains are not so grand.

When I am high up in the sky, I am in awe of all that I see, of all the things that God created and that man has built. My struggles fade into the background when I look upon the unending expanse of the sky.

When I fly, I know that I am at the mercy of this plane made of metal and bolts. I am humbled by my absolute lack of being able to control any single part of the process, while at the same time, I am absolutely amazed at the ability to travel such distances in such a short time.

Our verse says this:

"God looks down from heaven on all mankind to see if there are any who understand, any who seek God."

When He looks down from heaven, God, the maker of the entire universe, sees you.

When we look down from a plane, we see people moving around like little tiny specks. We cannot distinguish their eye color, their height, or their beliefs from such a high distance. God though, He can see the color of your eyes. He knows you so intimately that He *"knows the number of hairs on your head"* (Luke 12:7).

Not only does God know the details about how we look, but He also watches as we come and go.

Psalm 121:7-8 says this:

> *"The Lord will watch over*
> *your coming and going*
> *both now and forevermore."*

Though there are billions of people in this world, the Lord truly cares about each one.

Our verse says that:

> *"He is looking to see if there is anyone who*
> *understands God and seeks Him."*

God loves you and longs to have a personal relationship with you. He may allow things to come your way to get your attention, so that you seek Him in prayer and study His word. His only desire is that we seek His face, that we seek to know Him more and more.

Today as the Lord looks down on you, can you spend as much time studying Him through His word as you doing preparing yourself for your day?

Can you spend as much time talking to Him (praying) as you spend scrolling on social media?

As the sun sets on yet another day, can you have confidence that your time was spent wisely, that you have spent time seeking the Lord today for wisdom, peace, and understanding?

The Creator of the universe longs to have a relationship with us. Just as a pilot knows where and how to fly a plane to get us to our destination, let's be intentional about getting to know God deeper, more and more each day.

We don't know how many days we each have left to live, so let's be purposeful about living today, loving Jesus and growing closer to Him. You won't regret it!

First published October 29, 2020 at www.ibelieve.com

How to Overflow with Hope

Romans 15:13 - May the God of hope fill you will all joy and peace as you trust in him, so that you may overflow with hope by the power of the Holy Spirit.

When my girls were younger, they loved to play tea parties. They would lay out a fancy table cloth and set the table with their play tea set. They would fill the plates with treats from the kitchen, and then dress up in their princess gowns with plastic tiaras tilted on their heads. They layered on as much of their jewelry as they could, and happily clunked around the house in my heels. They excitedly invited me, along with all of their favorite dolls to feast at their tea party.

When they first began to host these tea parties, the tea party would be out on the patio or in the kitchen which had a tile floor. You see these little girls, in their efforts to be the best hostess, would pour and pour and pour their "tea" (water) into my tea cup. They poured so much water that the "tea" filled the cup, overflowing onto the saucer and dripping onto the tea table and sometimes to the floor. They were unable to figure out how to stop pouring when the cup reached its limit.

As the tea party hostesses grew, they continued to have elaborate tea parties with me, progressing eventually to real china and actual tea. By this time, they had learned how to fill the cup without overflowing it.

Our verse talks about hope. My girls had many hopes for their tea party. They wanted to feel pretty, all dressed up. They wanted to enjoy all the specialness that came along with playing hostess. They wanted to create a special moment for us.

In our lives we need hope. Hope is what we cling to, that promises that our tomorrow will be better, that things will somehow work out. Without hope we lose our focus and our strength to persevere.

This verse tells us that:

"God is our hope."

If we have a personal relationship with Him, then we can turn to Him at all times. When we turn to Him, trusting that He has things in control, then we can move through our days with joy and peace.

The interesting thing about our verse is that we must trust in Him first. *Then* He fills us with joy and peace. That in turn causes us to overflow with hope.

I need overflowing hope in the midst of my busyness, in the center of my struggles. I need overflowing hope more than ever before as I move into a new phase of my girls nearing high school graduation and my parents growing older.

We desperately need hope that overflows our lives, in the new struggles that the Coronavirus has brought to our lives. Job losses, financial struggles, illness, fear. This world needs to see this hope in you. This verse promises you so much hope, that it overflows and changes those around you!

Hebrews 6:18 says to:

> *"Hold fast to the hope set before you"*
> - Jesus is our hope!

Will you join me today in trusting Jesus a little more than yesterday, holding tightly to the hope that He has already given you, the hope of salvation, the promise that He will provide for you, the truth that He will never leave you or forsake you?

Can you trust that He will move and work in your life and through you today?

When my girls moved from their plastic tea set to my fine china, I reminded them to hold it tightly. I knew their little hearts would be devastated if they dropped it and it shattered.

So, their little fingers held it so tightly that their knuckles were white, yet their pinky was stinking out in the proper tea fashion (they thought).

As you hold onto the hope you already have, and are then filled with joy and peace as you completely trust Him for your circumstances, you better hold on tightly! God will begin to pour so much hope in you that it will overflow. Your life will certainly be changed by His hope, joy and peace.

First published November 3, 2020 at www.ibelieve.com

How to Get Rid of "All Such Things"

Colossians 3:8 - But now you must rid yourselves of all such things as these: anger, rage, malice, slander, and filthy language from your lips.

Almost three years ago my husband and I decided to downsize. At the time it seemed like a simple thing to do. It didn't seem to be a problem that downsizing meant we would move from a five-bedroom, four-bathroom house of 3,200 sq feet into a two-bedroom, one bathroom house of 896 sq feet. Now keep in mind that we also have two teenage daughters whom we homeschool (and all their belongings) as well as one very large, very active dog. This turned out to be the craziest adventure of my life!

Easy, I thought!

Then our large house sold quickly.

Since we had to move sooner than I planned, my super practical husband got a storage unit for six months. The plan was to just move our extra stuff into it, and then over those six months to sort through, sell, or give away what absolutely *could not fit* into our super small house with its teeny tiny closets. Basically, we had to rid ourselves of about 75% of our belongings.

Some things were super easy to get rid of. Extra clothes, linens, dishes, old furniture – not a problem. It was easy to donate books that we had outgrown or could get at the library. It was not so easy to get rid of knick knacks and other items that help sentimental value, even though, to be honest, I hadn't even looked at in the ten years we had been in that house.

Purging the things that I no longer needed, but was holding onto purely for the memories, was extremely hard. It hurt to give or to throw those things away. With a lifetime of memories and tokens though, I couldn't keep each one. There was literally no room, except for a few. I had to choose and each decision mattered.

Our verse gives us some pretty strong language. The first part says:

"But now you must rid yourselves of all such things as these: anger, rage, malice, slander, and filthy language from your lips."

This command is very clear about what we need to do. The Bible is telling us to get rid of the things which are not only hurting our testimony, but are also keeping us from knowing Christ more fully and walking in close fellowship with Him.

These issues of anger, rage, malice, slander, and filthy language are rampant in our society today. Sadly, it has become the norm for even Christians. Paul tells us to rid ourselves of them. This is not a "shove it in the back of the closet" command, or a "hold onto it in case you might need it" situation. Instead, Paul is exhorting us to throw it in a trash bag, tie it up, throw it in the car and drive it immediately to the dump, kind of action. Once it's in the dump, it is gone. It has no place in your life anymore. In its place we are to grow the fruit of the spirit: love, joy, peace, patience, kindness, goodness, faithfulness, gentleness, and self-control.

If we have the courage and the strength to get rid of all the anger, rage, malice, slander, and filthy language that lies in our hearts, think of all the peace that we would have. Think of all the freedom. Think of all the good that would come in our homes, our relationships, our hearts and our minds.

Getting rid of a lifetime of stuff was super hard, but I am now living more carefree.

Since I have purged my life of all the extra unnecessary items, I can now clean my entire house in under an hour! I have more time to do the things I love, without spending hours maintaining all my belongings.

Knowing there is no more room in the house for frivolous items has caused me to be extra careful about what comes through my door. The same thing holds true for us about what Paul wrote. Once we have rid ourselves of anger, rage, malice, slander, and filthy language, we will find that we don't want them to come back. We don't want to carry that burden anymore! We will be more intentional about our reactions to other people and to situations.

Will you join with me to rid ourselves of these things and intentionally replace them with the fruit of the Spirit? We can do this in the following simple moment by moment ways:

1. Make the decision to not allow the feelings of anger to enter before you face someone you struggle with.

2. Instead of flying into a rage when you get angry, pray for peace and forgiveness before, during and after your time with that person.

3. Pray for those who hurt you and forgive often. Do this, instead of holding malice or slandering someone on social media, to your husband or to your friend.

4. Pray for the Lord to guard your tongue and that your words would be pleasing to Him.

Stop listening to others swear, whether that be your friends, tv or music. Choose to fill your mind with words from the Bible. Remember "garbage in, garbage out."

Let's downsize the negative emotions from our lives, and move into freedom to love and live, reflecting Christ to the world around us today.

First published November 5, 2020 at www.ibelieve.com

God Will Not Fail You

Deuteronomy 31:6 - So be strong and courageous! Do not be afraid and do not panic before them. For the Lord your God will personally go ahead of you. He will neither fail you nor abandon you.

I was putting away our things one night, when I heard my daughter screaming from the garage. It was a blood-curdling scream, a scream with more terror than I had ever heard from my daughter ever! I ran to the garage, flung the door open and turned on the light. She stood there, white as a sheet, her little shoulders shaking as she sobbed.

"What is it?" I said, as I ran to her, throwing my arms around her in comfort.

"The light went off and I couldn't see." She sobbed.

The garage door opener light had been on when she had returned to the garage to get her book, but as it was on a timer, it had turned off, leaving her in darkness, and filling her with terror in its unexpectedness.

Change comes often.

We should expect it, but usually when it comes, we get thrown into a tizzy, surprised at its suddenness. This Coronavirus has left many in our world ragged. This is sudden. It has caused permanent changes to the way our days look. We question the value of each activity. Closures have happened all around, many permanent.

This is a change we were not expecting. This is a change that causes great fear in many people around the world. Fear of catching the virus, fear of our loved ones getting sick, fears of stores running out of essentials and fear of the financial ramifications.

As a mom, I have had many conversations lately with my children about not being afraid or panicking with all that is happening around us right now. I know that I must be strong before them, regardless of the thoughts of fear that are trying to knock at my heart and thoughts.

I love the truth in this verse:

"So be strong and courageous!
Do not be afraid
and do not panic before them.
For the Lord your God
will personally go ahead of you.
He will neither fail you nor abandon you."

Moses, the leader of Israel, spoke these words to his successor Joshua and to the people when they were preparing to face a very real enemy.

An enemy that they had to fight in order that they could have a place to live and worship as a free people. They didn't know that it would take many long years to fight their enemies.

As we continue to go about our days, with this virus still spreading all around the world, now is the time to put feet to our faith. We must remind ourselves and our children that God knows our tomorrows. We must remind ourselves that now is the time to trust Him even more.

Let's spend even more time in the Bible and reread all the times that God helped people, how He healed many, how He moved in spite of bad circumstances, and how He sustained His children during the suffering.

"For the Lord will personally go ahead of you. He will neither fail you nor abandon you."

He knows your days. He knows your finances. He knows your future.

Through all the changes our todays and tomorrows bring, He will not fail you and He will not abandon you during this time. He will continue to be with you. Let's trust Him through this pandemic, knowing that He will do something wonderful in our hearts, our homes and our testimonies.

First published November 10, 2020 at www.ibelieve.com

Prepare for the Battles Facing You

1 Samuel 17:47 - And everyone assembled here will know that the Lord rescues His people, but not with sword and spear. This is the Lord's battle, and He will give us to you.

One boy saved a nation. That same boy would later lead that nation as their king. Yet this boy, the youngest in his family, had probably been picked on by all his older brothers. When chores were divided up, he got the worst one - he had to take care of the sheep. This meant that he had to sleep near the sheep to ensure that they had good food and water. He had to tend to their illnesses. He had to protect them from wild animals. This was not a job for the lazy or weak. This job made a man of him while he was still a boy.

During this time his country, the nation of Israel, was faced with a very real enemy. An army had lined up to fight them. Their greatest soldier, who happened to be a giant, taunted them day and night. He mocked them and he mocked their God.

So, what did the Israelite soldiers do? They trembled in fear.

What did the Israelite king do? He hid in his tent and promised his daughter in marriage to any man who would step up and would fight that big bad guy.

Not one single man stepped forward. To agree to fight this giant would surely mean death. To lose would mean that the entire nation would become slaves to their enemy. The odds to fight were too great. So, all the soldiers waited, listening to their enemy taunting them, every single day, all day long.

Then one day this shepherd boy was sent to deliver food to his older brothers who were in the army. This boy couldn't believe his ears as he listened to this giant taunt them. So, this boy stepped up to fight.

You see, while this boy spent all his days alone watching over the sheep, he spent that time singing songs of worship to God.

He prayed to God, and spent many hours thinking about what God had done for him and his nation.

He reminded himself of how God had helped them in the past.

He knew that he could count on God and that God could count on him.

He was prepared for battle *before* he even got to the battlefield.

He ignored his brothers telling him to go home, and he approached the king. The king eagerly outfitted him with his own sword and shield. David declined and proceeded to face an enemy with only his staff, a sling and five smooth stones. The giant mocked him as David approached him. The giant threatened to kill him and feed his body to the birds and wild animals.

But David answered him this:

"Everyone assembled here will know that the Lord rescues His people, but not with sword and spear. This is the Lord's battle, and He will give us to you."

David put a rock into his sling, swung it and just like that the giant was dead.

This story points out some facts. All the stuff that we go through in our life, are stepping stones to us being able to endure harder things down the line. Easy is not guaranteed. I wish we could just fight our battles once and for all and then live on vacation the rest of our lives, but we can't.

The Israelites rushed to join the battle after David killed the giant. Sometimes in life we have to be the first to fight, to lead the way. The world is looking to Christians now more than ever as they are faced with their hopeless situations.

This wasn't the last battle that David and Israel had to face. They had many battles, with many different countries for many more years. David also faced personal battles in his home life as he struggled at times. One thing remained constant throughout his life. He needed God. He worshipped God and he didn't care who saw his dependence on God or his exuberant joy for trusting Him.

May this be an encouraging word to you. No matter what situation you are facing today, God is near you! He *will* rescue you!

If you have given Him your life, then He is the one who is going to battle for you. Let's keep our eyes on God through our battles. Let's show this struggling world how great our God is. Let's walk boldly into our battles, confident that God is with us, and that our giants will be defeated!

First published November 19, 2020 at www.ibelieve.com

What To Do When You Lose the Path

Psalm 119:105 - Your word is a lamp to my feet and light to my path.

While visiting Charlotte one fall, I had a few hours open one Sunday afternoon. I longed to be out walking in the crisp fall air, so I quickly googled hikes nearby. I saw that there was one nearby, but it would close at sunset, which was in three hours, so I didn't have a lot of time. I choose this hike for two reasons: limited crowds on a football Sunday, and all the reviews said that the path was well marked. I wanted to walk alone, but I wanted to know where I was going.

I checked in at the office and then found the trailhead. The fall foliage was breathtaking, and I slowly walked through the first ½ mile, snapping pictures of the leaves, and breathing in the fresh country air, finding peace after a busy week of work. I put away my camera, knowing that the park would eventually close and I still had a few more miles to walk.

The trail was easy to follow for some time, until suddenly it was not. The reviews had said that the trail was clear and easily marked. That may have been true in the summer, but with all the fallen leaves, I quickly lost sight of the trail. I stopped and looked around me. There was a blanket of leaves all over the ground. I looked up at the sky to gauge the setting sun. I had time, but I had to keep moving. I had to find the trail. I stood in one spot, but turned myself around, scanning for any sign of the trail. None. But wait, there was a tiny sign on a tree over to the side. I walked to it, and sure enough, there was an arrow with the word trail under it.

I continued my hike, following the directions from the small signs nailed to trees. Without those signs, I would have never been able to know where the path was. I would never have been able to get to the end of the trail in peace. I trusted those signs and they led me back to the parking lot.

It was a beautiful hike, and as I walked, I pondered this verse:

"Your word is a lamp to my feet
and a light to my path."

On that hike, I had a few choices when I lost sight of the trail: I could have stood and screamed until I was hoarse. I could have called 911. I could have ignored the signs pointing to the way.

Instead, I chose to trust the signs. I walked with my eyes looking for the next sign. They spoke truth and they got me back to my car in time to watch the sunset from the parking lot.

What decisions are you facing today that leave you lost, wondering which way to turn? Are you confused? Are you fearful? I have been, and I know that I will be again.

Life is hard. We make a decision to do something, thinking we will be fine, and then we lose sight of the trail, the sun sets, or we get lost. Situations keep coming at us that batter us, that leave us feeling like we are drowning.

However, we have this promise from the Bible that God's word will shed light on our next step, and will show us the path we are to follow. We have the choice though. We choose to open the Bible and seek God for each day's problems, or we can keep it closed and struggle on our own way. We always have a choice, in each situation, and through each day.

Joshua 24:15 says this:

"Choose for you this day whom you will serve."

Today will you choose to open the Bible and read a little bit of it?

Psalm 119:133 says this:

"Guide my steps by Your word."

Will you allow the Lord to guide your steps today?

The more we look to His word, the more clearly our spiritual eyes will see what He is doing in the midst of our circumstances and in our hearts.

Don't try walking the path of life alone, let Him be your hiking partner and walk the trail of life with you. What have you to lose?

First published June 2, 2020 at www.crosswalk.com

God Delights in Every Detail

Psalm 37:23-25 - The Lord directs the steps of the godly. He delights in every detail of their lives. Though they stumble, they will never fall, for the Lord holds them by the hand. Once I was young, and now I am old. Yet I have never seen the godly abandoned or their children begging bread.

As I prepared to be a first-time mom, I was obsessed with the details. I read books and searched the internet each week that I was pregnant, to not only see how big my baby was, but to learn how her body was miraculously changing. I read every new mom book I could get my hands on. I learned all about feeding and sleep schedules. I read reviews to buy the safest car seat, stroller and crib. I worried about every little detail before she even came.

Once my precious little girl arrived, the details didn't stop. In fact, they became even more a part of my thought process. Every cough, every different cry, became something I became very in tune with.

I worked through every detail of her new life.

Everything she ate, everything she touched, and every new thing that she did. It became normal for me to put her needs, her details before my own. Her life depended on my working out the details, so to speak.

When she began to crawl, more details came. We installed a baby gate at the top of the stairs and at the bottom, so she didn't roll down them. We searched for daycares and cross examined any babysitter who came over.

As she began to walk, I would hold her little hands so that she would not fall, until she could do it on her own. I guided her to smooth places to practice walking so that she would not stumble or hurt herself.

Our verse says that:

"God delights in every detail of your life."

He is watching over you. He sees your fears, your sadness, your pain. He sees your joys, your choices, your struggles.

Just as I prepared ahead of time for each new phase of my little daughter's life, God too is preparing a way for you in every one of your situations.

God is holding your hand through the ups and downs of your life.

As she took her first faltering steps, my little girl didn't see all the things that would be coming her way. She didn't know she would fall and hit her chin, requiring stitches, and leaving a scar. She didn't know that one day while running at the park she would trip, scraping her knee and leaving another scar. She didn't need to worry about any of that. If she had focused on what pain her tomorrows would bring, she might not have held my hands and taken her first steps.

In our life as Christians, as we try to trust God for each of our situations, we too stumble and fall. We too have scars from the pain that we have encountered.

God promises us that He will be with the godly. Who are they? They are the ones who seek Him by reading the scriptures for hope and direction. The godly are the ones that pray when happy and pray when desperate. The godly are the ones who go through each day, knowing that God is delighting in every single detail of their lives.

He isn't laughing when we hurt. He has a way through the hurt, and in the process, we will learn more about Him.

Let's live the rest of our lives, being a witness to the world of this hope:

"I have never seen the godly abandoned or their children begging bread." (Psalm 37:25)

Now is a good time to share hope and peace with the world. Let's live today, trusting God to delight in our details, and to hold us by the hand. We may stumble, but we will not fall. God said it. Let's start intentionally believing it and living it.

First published November 23, 2020 at www.crosswalk.com

Do Whatever It Takes

Mark 2:4 (NLT) - They couldn't bring him to Jesus because of the crowd, so they dug a hole through the roof above his head. Then they lowered the man on his mat, right down in front of Jesus.

I want friends like this man. Though his friends accepted his handicap, they loved him so much that they wanted better for him. They wanted him to dance at their weddings, walk in the fields with them, and discuss the scriptures on the way to worship.

His friends had heard about this man named Jesus who raised the dead, healed the sick, gave sight to the blind, and made the lame walk. They decided that today would be the day that their friend would be healed. Today their friend was going to walk.

They picked up their friend, lying on his mat and carried him over to the house where Jesus was.

The whole town appeared to have also shown up!

The friends stood there for a moment.

There was absolutely no way that they would be able to even get into the house as they viewed the huge crowd blocking the door.

They knew that they had to do something different. So up to the roof they went, cut a hole in the roof and lowered their friend down into the room and laid him at the feet of Jesus. There were no limits in their mind of them doing *whatever* it would take to bring their friend to Jesus.

I went through a season recently where I felt like I couldn't move, where each day was full of mental exhaustion and each night I tossed and turned, unable to sleep, drained emotionally from all that my days were bombarding me with. I would go to church, I would pray, I would read the Bible, deeply longing for a fresh touch from the Lord.

It was during this dry spiritual season that I met another lady at church. We decided to meet at the beach to walk and pray, lifting each other's needs before the Lord. To hear someone else bringing your needs before the Lord is truly heart-changing.

This new friend and I tried to do our prayer walk every couple of weeks for the rest of that school year.

As the weeks passed, my circumstances became resolved.

My faith grew fresher.

My prayers grew stronger.

My hope was being restored.

During these months, I continued to pray by myself, but having this new friend also beseech heaven for my needs, was so humbling, yet so incredibly powerful. It reminds me of this verse from Colossians 1:9-10:

"And so, from the day we heard,
we have not ceased to pray for you,
asking that you may be filled with
the knowledge of His will in all
spiritual wisdom and understanding,
so as to walk in a manner worthy of the Lord,
fully pleasing to Him,
bearing fruit in every good work
and increasing in the knowledge of God."

We need others to walk alongside us through the ups and downs of this life. We need others to bring us to the feet of Jesus.

I strongly believe the promise of these words found in Jeremiah 29:13:

"You will seek me and you will find me,
when you seek me with all your heart."

I do know that there are times of desperation, brokenness, and stress when we also need the strength of a faith friend to bring us to the feet of Jesus.

Moses needed Hur and Aarons hands holding his arms up during the battle. (Exodus 17:12)

Ruth and Naomi both needed each other to get through a very difficult season together. (Ruth)

The injured man desperately needed the Good Samaritan to carry him to a place of safety and healing.   (Luke 10:25-37)

The disciple Andrew brought his brother Peter to Jesus. (John 1:41)

Galatians 6:2 says that we are to:

> *"Carry each other's burdens and*
> *thus fulfill the law of Christ."*

Is there anyone in your life right now who needs you to come along and carry them to the feet of Jesus?

When someone is in the trenches of despair, sometimes just seeing a hand reaching out to them means all the difference in their lives physically and spiritually. Pray for the Lord to open your eyes to who He wants you to reach out to. It's very likely that many in your circle are hurting and need a fresh touch from Jesus.

Will you join me today in looking for someone whom you can bring to the feet of Jesus?

Let's be the ones who will do *whatever* in our efforts to restore lives and bring souls to the Lord today.

Those friends in our story damaged someone's roof to lay their friend at Jesus' feet. Their heart was in the right place, so I know that after their rejoicing party dance, that they also repaired that roof, their healed friend right at their side helping them make the roof brand new. Jesus' touch brings new roofs, fresh hearts and changed lives.

First published July 3, 2020 at www.ibelieve.com

How To Pray on All Occasions

Ephesians 6:18 - And pray in the Spirit on all occasions with all kinds of prayers and requests. With this in mind, be alert and always keep on praying for all the Lord's people.

It never fails. Every single time I open a package of meat, my dog will be right there at my side in less than five seconds. He can be in a deep sleep, in the other room or even outside on the porch. As soon as I begin to open any package of meat, he is right at my side or begging to come in, always in less than five seconds.

Sometimes, just for fun, I will start counting, one, two, three, four, five. I rarely even make it to the number five before he is right there beside me.

He has been known to push his way between me and the counter or the stove to get a closer whiff. His smell glands are so super-hyper that he will begin to bite at the air, trying to taste the meat. Once he even nudged me completely out of the way, just to get closer to the meat.

This happened once again last night, as I was frying some hamburger meat at the stove, the dog frantically sniffing at my side, when some questions went flying through my thoughts:

How fast do I turn to the Lord when my life gets stinky?

How quickly do I turn to Him for every situation or decision that comes my way?

How consistent am I in praying for others throughout my day?

Dogs need an acute smell system to help them find their food in the wild. It is critical to their survival. They don't need to practice at smelling meat. It is already deeply ingrained in them at birth. However, it isn't ingrained in us humans to pray at all times. Praying at all times and in all situations doesn't come naturally to us.

We are certainly quick to turn to the Lord when we have moments of crisis, when a need is urgent, or when a friend is rushed to the hospital.

We are certainly quick to keep on praying for their situation until they make a turn for the better.

The Bible verse though doesn't say to "pray to the Lord for help only when things are bad."

The words instead say:

> *"And pray in the Spirit on all occasions with all kinds of prayers and requests."*

What kinds of prayer can we pray throughout the day?

- Praying a variety of prayers ensures that we continue communicating with the Lord.

- Prayers of thankfulness for the way He is moving in our life.

- Prayers of praise for who He is.

- Prayers of mercy for our pain.

- Prayers of forgiveness for the intentional or unintentional sin we have committed.

- Prayers of warfare against Satan.

- Prayers for protection and provision.

Are you finding that you are quick to turn to the Lord only in times of need?

Praying for others throughout the day is not easy. It is something that we have to put into practice, repeatedly, until turning to the Lord is as natural to us as breathing. Who does the Lord bring to mind right now, as you read these words, that you can spend a moment praying for?

The verse tells us to be alert. When I walk into the kitchen to begin meal prep, my dog is on alert, watching me, waiting until he smells the meat before he appears right at my side in less than five seconds. As we move through our days, we are to be alert. We are to practice looking for situations so that we can bring them to the Lord in prayer.

As you drive down the street, pray for the people walking on the sidewalk, pray for the mail person, pray for that child walking their dog. God has put all these people in your line of sight, so why not pray for them?

Look around you right now. Who can you pray for? I look out my window and see the corner of my neighbor's house. I pray for that man. He needs God somehow, today. Maybe I am the only one praying for him.

Can you start to look for opportunities through your day and circumstances to pray?

Are you willing to teach yourself to be quick to respond to God in prayer in less than five seconds? You see someone, you pray. You remember someone, you pray.

Can you do this practice so often that it becomes ingrained in you, so that in every circumstance you are quick to pray, hopefully in less than five seconds? Try it today and see how it can change your life and the lives of those around you.

First published November 19, 2019 at www.ibelieve.com

I Am and I Will

Isaiah 41:10 - So do not fear, for I am with you; do not be dismayed, for I am your God. I will strengthen you and help you; I will uphold you with my righteous right hand.

I walked into the house and over to the kitchen. I dropped the car keys and my purse on the counter, crossing over to the sink to get a drink of water. My legs collapsed under me and I sank to the ground. There was a loud whooshing sound in my ears. My heart was beating so hard that I thought it would break my chest wide open. I drew my knees up to me and wrapped my arms around my legs, gasping for breath. I do not know how long I sat there on the tile floor, but I know that it was a very long time. As my heart began to slow to a regular beat and I was able to take a normal breath of air, I slowly stood to my feet.

Time seemed to have stood still in my heart and mind, so I was surprised to see that the early winter sunset had arrived. Time had passed without me having any knowledge of it. I realized that this had been a panic attack.

Earlier that day I had kissed my husband goodbye as he left to board a plane. He was being deployed to Iraq. He was being sent there to serve our country, to be in an area where our contact would be very limited. I knew he had to go, but it was one of the hardest things I have ever experienced.

I tried to control my thoughts as I was in the midst of that panic attack, trying to gain control over my fears. I was absolutely terrified that I would never see my husband again, that I would have to raise our daughter alone. As I sat on that cold tile floor, with my arms wrapped around my legs, I focused very hard on telling myself the truth with each struggling breath. I was not alone. God was with me.

God promises this to us:

> *"He will never leave me nor forsake (abandon) me."* (Deuteronomy 31:6)

> *"I can do all things through Christ who gives me strength."* (Philippians 4:13)

Through the weeks and months that followed I was able to get through each day, to pray through my fears, and my worry.

I never had a panic attack like that again through the years, but there are still times that I struggle with anxiety, when my life gets a bit full of life's stuff. It is in those moments of struggle that I must speak truth to my heart, my mind and my circumstances.

Sometimes I even need the truth spoken to me by a loved one. It's also during those times that I find myself craving to read the Bible, to help me remember God's promises.

I love this Bible verse because it shows that God truly loves us. He knows that we experience fear, and that we are often dismayed by the circumstances in our life.

He knows that only in Him can we find the strength to carry on.

He says: *"I will strengthen you and help you."*

He knows that we cannot do this life and our battles alone.

He also says:

"I will uphold you with my righteous right hand."

The right hand of God signifies His favor and His strength in your circumstances.

So whatever situation you are struggling with today, remind yourselves of the truths from this Bible verse:

GOD says: I am with you
             I am your God
             I will strengthen you
             I will help you
             I will uphold you with my righteous right hand (God's strength)

You say: I will not allow my fear to overtake me
             I will not be dismayed by my problems
             God is with me
             God is strengthening me
             God is helping me
             God is holding me up with His righteous, strong right hand

You can get through this situation of trouble because GOD is with you, holding you up. Picture someone walking into an emergency room, leaning on someone stronger to get them to a place of refuge, of help. That is exactly you and God. He is holding you up through each moment and He will *not* let this situation destroy you.

First published March 25, 2020 at www.ibelieve.com

God is My Guide

Psalm 48:14 - For this God is our guide for ever and ever; He will be our guide even to the end.

While on a vacation to Ecuador, my husband, our two daughters and myself enjoyed all the sights, sounds and experiences of a different culture.

We enjoyed walking around the city that we were staying in, trying out the different restaurants and exploring the city's historic buildings.

One day we stumbled upon a local equestrian school that also gave trail rides. To my girl's great excitement, we made plans for a two hour ride the next day.

Our trail guide spoke English and matched us up with horses whose temperaments balanced our inexperience.

Our guide then led us down dirt roads, crossing small creeks, then passing by farms of sheep, horses and cattle. We saw women hanging out their laundry, and men working in their fields.

The Ecuadorian countryside was so peaceful and quiet. Our guide would talk with us throughout the entire ride, pointing out how to ride better, what we should look at across the road, and encouraging us for how we were controlling the horses. Our experience was so amazing, and our trust in the guide so strong, that when he mentioned a more difficult trail ride that he thought that we should do, we agreed and booked the ride for the next week.

The day before our second trail ride was stormy, raining all day long. My girls were very worried that our trail ride would be cancelled, but the next day the sun peeked out from the clouds, promising to be a beautiful day.

We began our trail ride through a grassy field, and then stopped at the base of a mountain. Our guide said that the trail was narrow and muddy and that his horses knew how to handle the ride up and down, so we were just to keep our hands loose on the reins. Our guide kept telling us to trust the horses when the path was muddy, so we did.

The horses did easily climb to the top of the Andes Mountain. The view was absolutely breathtaking.

That need for trust soon became crucial again as the horses began to descend down the mountain.

The trail was steep and very muddy. My youngest daughter rode in front of me. I began to freak out as I saw her horse lose its footing and start to slip down the path. My horse also began to slip as it followed closely behind her. The guide yelled out a reminder to us to let the reins lose and let the horse get us down the hill safely.

Though it went against my need to control this situation, I trusted the guide and loosened my hands. My horse quickly found solid footing, but I couldn't breathe easily until we were back on flat ground.

"For this God is our guide forever and ever;
He will be our guide even to the end."
(Psalm 48:14)

I love this Bible verse! I can't read it without thinking of how important trust in my trial guide and horse were vital to our experience.

This is our God.

We never need to doubt who God is. He is God, always and forever. He will be our guide.

I love the way the writer uses the phrase: *"for ever and ever."* He was emphasizing that God will guide us, and He will not stop guiding us ever!

The verse also says:

"He will be our guide to the end."

I love that I can spend the rest of my life allowing God to lead me to truth, and to places, experiences and relationships because I am trusting Him. I can trust Him because I am seeking to know Him more.

It's only when we have built that experience of trust in Him that we can allow ourselves to trust that He will guide us in every situation that we are going through.

Have you accepted this God as your God?

As you go through new experiences, are you remembering how He helped you through other situations in the past?

It's only when we intentionally get to know this God, and allow our trust in Him to grow, that we can have stronger faith to get through the muddy, slippery paths of our life.

The more we know Him, the more we can trust Him to not let us fall. Today I pray you will trust this God to guide you forever and ever, and that He will be your guide to the very end.

First published November 14, 2019 at www.ibelieve.com

Old Age and Gray Hairs

Isaiah 46:4 - Even to your old age and gray hairs I am He, I am He who will sustain you. I have made you and I will carry you; I will sustain you and I will rescue you.

My grandmother lived a very long life. Many of my childhood memories include my mom, siblings and I visiting her in a retirement home. She and my mother would talk for hours about the Bible and current world events.

My grandmother was intelligent and quick to give insights about things happening around the world, none of which interested me then. I preferred to hear her talk about her father, who had been a Baptist preacher. I liked to hear stories of her childhood, of how the people in her church thought that playing cards, going to the movies, and wearing lipstick was scandalous for Christians back in the 1920's.

In the last few years of my grandmother's life, she slipped into the grip of dementia, reaching a point where the only person she recognized was my dad. She became angry that she couldn't remember us.

Sometimes she would tell us to go away, her voice mumbling about people trying to pretend to know her. Eventually her dementia was so strong that she would mumble incoherently. She also became bedridden and completely blind.

Somewhere along the way we discovered the key to making our time with her peaceful. We found that if we opened the Bible and read sections of it aloud, that she would calm down. We noticed that when we read from the King James Version, that she would follow along, reciting the words that she had once learned so very long ago. Our visits to her became mostly Bible reading sessions, and singing old hymns. My grandmother's warbly voice would strengthen as she would sing the songs. Though the years had taken away her memory of us, the words of God were tucked so very deeply into her soul, that she could recall them quickly and with ease.

I love that this verse mentions our:

"Old age and our gray hair."

No one is exempt from that. It will bring aches and pains. It will diminish our eyesight and hearing. Our bones will become fragile, our muscles weaker. Our hair will gray or become white. We will eventually give up trying to dye it to its once youthful hue.

In all this: *"God will sustain us."*

He will keep us going. He will carry us. He will rescue us. I love how God mentions that He will sustain us two times in this short verse. How do you need God to sustain you today?

How does God sustain us? One way is through His Word. He gives us spiritual strength when we spend time in His Word.

My grandmother spent her childhood growing up in church. She memorized the scriptures and she heard her father preach the Word from the pulpit. She learned the hymns by singing the songs each Sunday. As an adult she spent hours studying the Bible on her own. When her eyes grew dim and she could no longer read, we read to her. The familiar words were a balm to her soul and emotions, it brought her tremendous peace.

If we don't know God, it's difficult to trust Him. It's hard to see how He can sustain us through the ups and downs of our lives if we haven't memorized His words of promise.

Are you memorizing scripture, planting it deep into your soul? The Bible does no good to you if it sits unopened on a bookshelf. It is meant to be read, to be studied, to be applied to your life.

Have you accepted Jesus in your life as your Savior? If you haven't, what is stopping you from doing so?

Do you make a concentrated effort to be in His Word, getting to know Him on a deeper level on a consistent (daily) basis? If you don't, what can you do to make that a part of your day?

We live in such an amazing time. Many of us have more Bibles in our house than people! We can also access the Bible digitally so that we can listen to it on our drive home or while we are doing odd jobs around the house. We can tune into radio stations, or turn on YouTube to hear the hymns and other songs about God. Let us never become immune to having access to the Bible, but let us be intentional about accessing it to change our life.

God made you. He wants to sustain you. He wants to rescue you. He wants to carry you. Get to know Him through His words, and allow Him to sustain you not only today, but through the years to come, all the way to your old age and your very last hair has turned gray.

First published November 21, 2019 at www.ibelieve.com

God Is and God Will

Daniel 3:16b &17 - We have no need to answer you in this matter. If this be so, our God whom we serve is able to deliver us from the burning fiery furnace, and he will deliver us out of your hand, O King.

Shadrach, Meshach and Abednego only wanted to live their lives and never asked for trouble to come looking for them. Trouble came anyway. These three had been brought as young men to Babylon as war captives. They excelled at their work, and were appointed to leadership over the province of Babylon. However, some men, who were close to the King, hated these three men for one reason: Shadrach, Meshach and Abednego were Jews.

In an effort to remove them from power, the evil tattle-tellers noticed that these three did not obey the command from the king of the land: to bow down before the statue of the king. Bowing down to anything was an act of worship, and they desired to obey God above man, even though they lived in a country where God was not honored or even worshipped.

When the King asked them about it, (and threatened them with the fiery furnace) they replied:

"We have no need to answer you in this matter.
If this be so, our God
whom we serve
is able to deliver us
from the burning fiery furnace,
and He will deliver us out of your hand, O King."

The King was furious and had the heat turned up in the fiery furnace 7 times hotter, then commanded the guards to throw these men in.

As they were arrested, tied up and carried toward the furnace, they heard the fires crack, they felt the intense heat, and yet they still believed in their God.

Due to the overwhelming heat, the guards died as they drew close, dropping Shadrach, Meshach and Abednego into the furnace.

These three men believed that God was able to deliver them before they got into the fire, but if not, that God would deliver them from the fire. They knew that nothing was impossible with God. He would deliver them. They were confident of that.

It continues in the story to say that everyone now can see four men (one with the face of a God) walking around in the fire! In astonishment the king commanded the men to come out of the fire.

There are a few things that this story tells us:

1. Sometimes God delivers us before the trouble, sometimes He delivers us while we are in trouble.

God had the power to prevent this situation from happening. He had a purpose for revealing His power.

Can you trust Him to work in you and your troubles?

2. We always have a choice in our faith.

At any point these men could have questioned how important it was to take a stand. They had been given plenty of time to recant what they believed.

In the trouble you might find yourself in, can you hold true to God even if He doesn't show up in your timing?

3. If we are walking with the Lord, the troubles will not linger around us.

These guys came out of this intense furnace intact. Not one burn at all! Not even the smell of smoke on them!

In the troubles you are walking through in faith, you will not be consumed by them. They will not linger or cripple you! You will emerge stronger than ever. Don't give up!

4. We are honored for our unwavering faith.

These men did not waver in their faith. It amazed the king. He worshipped God, and made a law that no one could dishonor God again. He then promoted Shadrach, Meshach and Abednego. God honored these men for their faith and trust in Him, and rewarded them in their careers.

Cling to what you know to be true about the Lord. He will honor you for it! Don't for one tiny moment even doubt the work of God in your life and your circumstances. He is most certainly at work in all of your troubles!

This story is so encouraging to me, and certainly strengthens my faith. Will you join with me today in saying:

"Our God is able to deliver me from this trouble, and He will deliver me, but if not, I will not serve any other god?"

May we be found faithful in our walk with the Lord this very day.

First published March 18, 2020 at www.ibelieve.com

Walking With God

Micah 6:8 - He has told you, O man, what is good; and what does the Lord require of you but to do justice, and to love kindness, and to walk humbly with your God?

One of the most amazing milestones to witness in a child's life is them learning to walk. They spend months strengthening arm muscles and leg muscles as they crawl around. Then, they discover that they can pull themselves up to stand. As their strength and confidence grow, they begin to walk themselves around the coffee table, holding onto the edge for balance. Finally, the day arrives when they will take their first faltering steps toward a proud parent or grandparent's outstretched arms. Both of my girls fell down after their first one or two steps, but were quickly scooped up and exuberantly praised for their success. After that moment, they were unstoppable in their new found freedom and their walking continuously improved.

When the day finally came that they were able to walk outside the safety of our house, I always held their hand so that they could walk right by my side, until they became mature enough to walk by me on their own.

Today, though they are now teenagers, my girls continue to walk by my side, engaging in conversation. When walking, if one lags behind, the other person always stops and waits for them to catch up. As we walk, they share their deep thoughts and struggles and we sort through it together.

I love the words this Bible verse in Micah uses when it tells us to:

"Walk humbly with our God."

To walk humbly simply means that we let God be God and let Him be the one in charge. We trust Him to walk beside us, guiding us and leading us according to His plan for our life.

I love that it says for us to walk *with* Him. We are walking at His side, not behind or in front of Him. As we walk by His side, we can learn from Him. We can grow in relationship with Him. It's an intentional action that we can take in our faith walk.

After her first step, my daughter was not able to walk around the block, let alone go on a hike in the mountains. She had to practice at her walk and get strong enough to get where she is today.

The more we choose to walk with the Lord, the easier our steps will be, the further our faith journey with Him.

The Bible speaks of several people who "walked" with God. Adam and Eve used to walk with God in the cool evening, until they chose to walk away from Him. The Bible also mentions that Abraham, Noah and Enoch walked with God, growing in relationship and knowledge of Him. As they walked with God through the years, they learned from Him about true justice, how to love kindness, and about humility. The Bible speaks of their faith, and their reliance on God. These men didn't choose to walk with God every so often, or just when it was convenient. They chose to do it daily, every single moment through the easy days, and definitely through the hard days.

Abraham, Noah, and Enoch weren't born as great men of faith. They learned to walk with faltering faith steps through each and every situation that came their way. They chose to walk beside Him through the thick and thin of life and therefore these men got through some pretty tough circumstances.

None of us has a perfect life. Each of us has experienced heartbreak, sickness, failure.

We live in a sinful world, so none of that pain will ever disappear, but as we journey through it, God will not leave our side. He says:

"I will never leave you." (Hebrews 13:5)

He wants to walk by us.

Joshua 1:9 says:

"Be strong and of good courage; do not be afraid, nor be dismayed, for the Lord your God is with you wherever you go."

No matter where you are in your faith journey today, know that you are not alone. The Lord is with you. Allow yourself to turn to Him, to seek His guidance for each of your situations.

Just as I dropped everything to stretch out my arms for my daughters' first faltering steps toward me, the Lord is standing before you, stretching out His loving arms, longing for you to turn to Him, to walk with Him, as you go through you days.

Today can you try walking with Him, asking Him for direction and peace as you go through your moments?

He wants to catch you when you fall.

He wants to guide you over the rough bumps on the path.

He wants to hear your dreams, your heartaches, your longings.

He is waiting to walk with you right now. So put on your walking shoes. Take a walk with God.

First published June 8, 2020 at www.crosswalk.com

Learning to Have Faith in Life's Storm

Psalm 61:4 - I long to dwell in your tent forever and take refuge in the shelter of your wings.

One fall, during my teens, my family went tent camping. We set up our camp and enjoyed hiking, playing card games, and cooking smores over the fire at night.

We didn't want to leave that Sunday evening, so my parents decided that my mom, sister and I would stay one more night. My brother and dad returned to our home in the city forty-five minutes away to work the next day. They would return Monday night to pick us up to end the camping trip.

That night we played games at the table by the glow of the lantern before heading to the tent to sleep.

At some point during the night, an intense thunderstorm descended upon us.

The wind grew stronger and stronger as our tent bent crazily under its force.

The thunderclaps deeply shook us, and lightning bolts lit up the sky as the storm dumped its fury all around.

My mom began to pray out loud for protection, not stopping through the long night, as the storm raged on around us.

The storm eventually passed.

We emerged from our tent to discover an empty campground. All the other campers had packed up and left during the storm's fury. Though tired from the night adventure, we had survived the storm in the shelter of our tent.

When the park ranger drove around the campground, inspecting the damage, he was amazed that our tent had withstood the storm and that we had remained dry inside it, as it was one of the worst storms that he had seen, with many campsites flooded or damaged with fallen tree branches.

Before our trip, my parents had made sure that they had bought a quality material tent. When they had set the tent up, they had chosen a location in a clearing between the trees and they had made sure that the tent stakes were pounded deep into the ground to hold that tent secure. Their preparation help minimize damage.

The one predictable thing in life is that we will experience many storms. Situations will come at us in intensity, the winds of fear and uncertainty pounding relentlessly, until we are tired and worn down.

The writer of our verse today is overwhelmed with troubles in his life. David was far from home, and feared for his safety, for his very life. He has been on the run for many years and was beyond weary from living on the run, expecting danger around every corner. He does the only thing that he can do in his dire situation. He pours out his desperate prayer to God. He longs to dwell in God's tent, and to take refuge in the shelter of God's wings. David wants to be safe, secure, and at peace.

What storms are raging around in your life today?

Are you desperate for some relief?

Are you gasping for breath, from the exhaustion of trying to hang on for just one more day?

As a child in that tent, I admit I was fearful, but I heard my mother's prayers, and I trusted that the tent would stay standing, that we would stay dry in its shelter. We were desperate for the storm to end, and in that desperation, we prayed ourselves through the storm.

Have faith, lift your troubles up to the Lord, leave them at His feet. Hide in the shelter of His wings. He loves you and longs for you to be desperate for Him. He wants to protect you and keep you safe in His tent.

Will you join me in refocusing our eyes on Him today? Let's pour our hearts out to Him, hand our fears over to Him, and rest in peace knowing that He is with us in the storms we are enduring today.

He will not leave us when the storm is at its worst. He will be with us before, during and after the storms. He will strengthen us through it all.

He has many things to reveal to us in the storms that He wouldn't be able to if we didn't walk through the storms with Him.

May the end of your storm find you being able to testify to others about how God was with you and brought you through. The storms are not about destroying you, but about building you.

Let's be desperate for God together, today. We don't want to ever go through a storm without Him with us. Lord, we long to dwell in your tent forever and take refuge in the shelter of your wings.

First published March 26, 2020 at www.ibelieve.com

Fix Your Eyes on Jesus

Hebrews 12:2 - Let us fix our eyes upon Jesus, the author and perfecter of our faith, who for the joy set before Him endured the cross, scorning its shame, and sat down at the right hand of the throne of God.

One warm summer day, my husband and I rented a 22-foot sailboat for a couple of hours to enjoy some time together in the San Diego Bay. He took his spot at the stern of the boat to steer the rudder, and I took my place up toward the middle so that I could manage the two sails. We enjoyed turning our boat and allowing the sails to catch the breeze to move us along at a dead run.

Partway through our time, we switched positions. I put my right hand on the rudder and my eyes on a point ahead in the distance. It was at this point it became my main responsibility to keep us on our current path. I had to keep the boat aligned with that distant object as my waypoint. If I took my eyes away from that waypoint, I could easily get us off course within seconds.

It would be dangerous for me to lose sight of that waypoint. Not only were there other boats in the water with us, but there was the shore, rocks and a bridge we could crash into. When we finally turned the boat around to head back to the marina, we once again chose a distant point for our eyes to focus on, to keep us on course.

That day in the sailboat I began to think about this verse:

"Let us fix our eyes upon Jesus,
the author and perfecter of our faith."

To fix my eyes upon Jesus is not a one-time deal. I must make that effort each and every moment, and in every single circumstance of my life in my personal walk with the Lord, to fix my eyes on Him and to not look away. I must allow Jesus to write His story in my life and allow Him to perfect my faith.

This definitely requires an effort on my part to always keep redirecting my course, to stay in tune with living for Him, by following His example through His life and teachings. How do I do this? The more that I spend time in the Word learning about Jesus, the easier it will be to keep my eyes on Him, no matter what.

The fog rolls in and the storms do come in life, and it sometimes seems as though I can't even see Jesus in the midst of my circumstances.

Those are the times when I have to press forward in faith, reminding myself that He is still there. I must intentionally fix my eyes on Jesus.

The Bible verse continues by saying:

"Who for the joy set before him endured the cross, scorning its shame, and sat down at the right hand of the throne of God."

Jesus endured so much on that cross. He did it for you. His love for you put Him on that cross. He endured it. He scorned the shame of the cross. He hated it.

We know He did it for love, but how did He do this?

He did it by intentionally setting joy before Him. He put His focus on the joy that He would receive at the end of it, which was to sit down at the right hand of God in Heaven.

No matter what situation you are in at this very moment, you must do all that is in your power to fix your eyes on Jesus through it. Don't take your eyes off of Him.

Remind yourself of His promises to you in the Bible.

Speak His truth into your life. He has a purpose for everything that you are going through right now.

There will be storms; there will be times of peace. Through your days, fix your eyes on Jesus and purposefully set joy before you. There is the promise of heaven, of peace at the end of our trials, of one day standing before the very throne of God. Don't ever quit fixing your eyes on Jesus. He is your waypoint!

First published October 14, 2019 at www.ibelieve.com

God Shows, Teaches and Guides Me

Psalm 25:4-5 - Show me your ways, LORD, teach me your paths. Guide me in your truth and teach me, for you are God my Saviour, and my hope is in you all day long.

When the hospital laid my newborn daughter in my arms, my heart overflowed with such awe. In the days that followed I watched in amazement as she began to interact more with her environment. The next few months brought an incredible amount of changes in her. Soon she could lift her head, turn over, sit up, hold her bottle, and feed herself finger food. All of these changes were innate within her.

Then the day came when I had to actually teach her how to do things, such as how to hold a fork, button a shirt, tie her shoes, or ride a bike. These things were not easy for her to learn, but they were an important part of her gaining independence and confidence. I needed to use a patient tone, and gentle hands to help guide her through the process. All these situations required repetition and practice on a daily basis until she could do it completely on her own.

When my daughter needed to learn to tie her shoes correctly, I would show her while I tied my shoes, explaining each thing that I was doing. Then I would guide her hands to tie her shoes, while using my words to talk her through each step that we were doing. My showing and teaching her this skill will be something that she will never forget. It is something that she can now do from memory.

I love how David used specific words when he was praying to God. He said:

"Show me and teach me."

He then used the words:

"Guide me and teach me."

David knew that truth from faith and personal experience. He needed God to show Himself, show him which way to go, and show His grace and mercy over and over again.

We need that truth as well, because we tend to forget way too quickly.

We need Him to teach us more about Him but also more about ourselves.

We must see how much we truly need Him in every part of our life.

The more we can allow God to show us His truth, the more it gets ingrained in us so that the next time difficulties come, our faith is stronger and we can endure it with a bit more strength and grace.

The next words from that verse that David uses is:

"Guide me in your truth and teach me."

He had so many troubles in His life, but David knew that he needed to be in God's word, meditating on His promises and seeking His direction. The more we know of God, the more that knowledge can guide us through our situations and circumstances.

When David penned those words, he was not writing them from a place of asking God to simply show, guide and teach him in his current difficult situation. He was asking the Lord to continually help him walk through his days. He wanted God to guide him with true wisdom that he could use for the rest of his life. Twice he asked God to teach him. He knew his own lack of knowledge. He knew how much he needed God. He desperately wanted God to be a part of his every moment. He knew that God must keep on teaching him, through showing and guiding him every day.

If you allow Him, God will continually move in your life as he did for David. Are you willing to let God show and teach you about yourself, about your situation, about His power in your life?

Are you willing to allow God to guide and teach you through your circumstance to grow stronger in your faith and your influence in the lives of those around you?

By allowing God to show, guide and teach you, it will allow your hope to rest in God all day long. Without hope, the day will be long and weary.

Why not allow Him to show Himself strong in your life, teaching you and guiding you in His truth?

First published November 12, 2019 at www.ibelieve.com

An Undivided Heart

Psalm 86:11 - Teach me your way, Lord, that I may rely on your faithfulness; give me an undivided heart, that I may fear your name.

One of the hardest things I have had to help my children work through is distractions. They are easily distracted while doing their schoolwork, their chores, and even in their conversations. They start out doing a task very focused, but then something happens to pull their mind away. The dog barking, a phone call, the dream they remembered from last night, things that they have to tell me about right now before they forget (even though they were supposed to be taking a math test).

The interesting thing is that when they are watching one of their TV shows or YouTube videos, their attention is focused. It is extremely hard to pull their gaze off the screen. When I do get their attention, they usually forget what I had told them later on. They sometimes have no recollection of what goes on around them or any idea of passing time, while focused on their show.

It all comes down to what they love. History book, versus an interesting novel. Two completely different attention spans. Two completely different results.

Our Bible verse today is a written prayer to the Lord for undivided attention. The author knew how hard it is to stay focused on what really matters, knowing the Lord. Just as my children are easily distracted while at work, I am as well while spending time in the Word or at prayer. My mind quickly wanders from the most important task at hand, being with Jesus.

It gives me encouragement to read these words written long ago. I know that I cannot have an undivided heart for the Lord without His help. I need Him to teach me how to stay focused on Him. The Bible verse makes it very clear that we cannot rely on His faithfulness, fear His name or have an undivided heart if we are not open to the Lord teaching us His way.

I have been teaching my children to set a timer, to remove distractions, and to intentionally work at staying focused while doing their schoolwork or chores. They have steadily gained progress as they have applied themselves to being focused.

How undivided is your heart for the Lord?

Are you faithful in the Word and in prayer?

Just as the writer of our verse wrote thousands of years ago, this struggle is not new, but I think the struggle is even harder today. Our lives are so incredibly busy and packed with activities, deadlines, and distractions, that if we even get to a quiet time, it's often a rushed moment, a thing to check off.

So, the writer of our verse knew that the secret to having an undivided heart is desire. He pleaded with the Lord to help him with this area because it was just too hard to do it all by himself.

Do you eagerly read the Word to learn from the Lord? Or has it become just another to-do item? Or perhaps it has even slid to the "do it later" pile?

Now is the day, now is the moment to make that decision about your heart. Is it divided or undivided? Are you okay with the answer to that question?

If you are serious about wanting to know the Lord more, about allowing Him to teach you what an undivided heart means, will you ask Him?

Will you join me in refocusing your mind and your schedule on the Lord?

Will you join me in being intentional about really growing closer to Him?

Look around you today. Everywhere you look, people are on their phones, barely taking their eyes off it as they walk or work. Every time you look at your phone, think of the Lord, say a prayer. Every time you open an email on your phone, also open the Bible app and ask the Lord to teach you something from the verse you read.

Just as I will wait today for my children to finish their schoolwork so that I can grade it, the Lord is waiting for us to talk with Him, to spend time in the Word learning all about Him. As a teacher, I don't want to wait all day for them to finish. As for our heavenly Father, I know He wants to hear from you sooner than later. He loves you and has so many things He wants to share with you. Don't put off until later the one thing that can make your life better. Time with Jesus, in His word and praying with Him will never be wasted time.

First published January 20, 2020 at www.ibelieve.com

Generous Living

Proverbs 22:9 - Whoever has a bountiful eye will be blessed, for he shares his bread with the poor.

I was newly married when I got my first dog. We named him Buddy, and he was super sweet and friendly.

We had a dog door that Buddy could access to go in and out of the house. One day I was at work in our office. I heard the dog door flap open then close as Buddy went outside. He enjoyed wandering around, digging little holes and checking to see if any of the neighbors were in their yard (for they were good for extra petting and sometimes a bone).

I had just finished my work in the office and was walking into the living room when Buddy poked his head in the dog door, looking around, to see what was going on. He saw me, leaped through the dog door and ran over to where I stood, dropping a dead bird at my feet. He stood there with his ridiculous grin, his tail wagging furiously with joy.

Two completely opposite thoughts ran through my brain at that moment. Gross. Blessed. There was a dead bird laying on my carpet where my little girls played. Disgusting. Then I looked at Buddy's grinning face. I knew that he loved me. He wanted to bless me by bringing me what he thought was an amazing gift. How could I be mad at that face, at that loving gesture?

I knelt down, gave him a big hug and said "good boy!" I then gave him a treat to distract him before grabbing some paper towels, picking up that dead bird and putting it in the trash. As I used cleaner to scrub the floor where the decaying bird had dropped, Buddy stood by my side sniffing around for the gift he had given me.

Over the years I have often thought of Buddy's generosity. All he wanted was to bless me instead of keeping that treasure for himself. In return, he was blessed with a hug, praise and a treat because he chose to give.

In our verse today, it says that whoever has a bountiful eye will be blessed. Buddy went out in the yard to explore and look for new things. He found a bird and thought of me.

As you go about your day, are you looking for opportunities to be generous?

Can you make it a point today to look for one person you can bless?

There are four habits of a bountiful person:

1. *A bountiful person gives generously.*

Buddy gave me the whole bird, keeping none for himself.

How can you be more generous to the people around you today?

2. *A bountiful person shares his faith.*

Who can you share God's love with? To whom can you give a Bible? What ministry can you donate some of your vacation days to helping?

3. *A bountiful person gives from his energy.*

Is there someone who needs a smile? Can you hold the door open for the tired mother and her crying toddler? Can you offer to watch someone's kids for a few hours so that they can have a break? Can you drive your elderly neighbor to the store to help them get groceries?

4. *A bountiful person gives his time.*

Can you carve out a few hours a month to help serve at the homeless shelter, or visit the elderly from your church who can't make it to services?

Our verse also says:

*"You will be blessed if you share
your bread with the poor."*

That bird would have been a sweet treat for Buddy, but he chose to share it with me.

Who can you share your bread with today?

Who can you bless out of the resources that the Lord has blessed you with?

When we choose to look for opportunities to bless others, we will be blessed in return.

Maybe the blessing will be that our perspective changes as we learn to live out our faith with those around us.

Maybe the blessing we receive is not tangible, but instead is just learning to live abundantly. Today, go out and look for one person to bless. See what a difference it will make in your heart and life.

First published January 22, 2020 at www.ibelieve.com

How to Be Deeply Rooted in Christ

Colossians 2:7 (NLT) - Let your roots grow down into Him, and let your lives be built on Him. Then your faith will grow strong in the truth you were taught, and you will overflow with thankfulness.

One weekend evening, many years ago, my family had been invited to dinner at a church member's home. I remember it as having been a fun, relaxing evening of good food and the chance for my brother, sister and I to enjoy playing new board games together as the adults talked in the other room.

The light afternoon rain had turned into a steady evening drizzle, with lighting and thunder increasing in their intensity. My parents began to worry about the road conditions and hurried us to clean up the games.

After saying our quick goodbyes, my dad pulled our car out of their driveway and turned down the road, heading to where we lived in an adjoining town, thirty minutes away. It was a two-lane, dark country road. The only light came from our headlights and the steady lightning in the sky around us.

My dad drove slower and slower down the road, the heavy rain quickly diminishing our visibility. Suddenly we all gasped. My dad quickly applied the brakes. Ahead of us, blocking the entire road was a huge tree. It had been uprooted and had fallen down. Our car stopped just inches from hitting it.

Slowly, carefully, my dad turned the car around and drove back a few miles to take a different road to get to our house. Thankfully no other trees fell to block our path, and we were able to get safely home.

As believers in Jesus, this verse reminds us to put down deep roots into Him, and let our lives be built on Him. That tree that fell down, lay across the road, all its roots were pulled up, exposed. The ground could not hold it because the tree had not allowed its roots to grow deep down into the ground through the years.

A tree depends upon its roots for food on a daily basis. If a drought came, the tree would eventually die from lack of nourishment. So too, our spiritual lives wither a little bit more every day that we spend away from having that focused time with God.

When you look honestly at your walk with the Lord, are you spending time in the Word?

Are you daily seeking to know Him more?

A tree also needs the roots to grow down deeper every single season, so that as the tree grows upward to maturity, the roots will be able to hold it in the ground, no matter how big that tree grows. This is also true in our faith. The more we know of the character of the Lord, the more we will begin to reflect Him as we live out our lives.

As we daily continue to spend time in the Word, learning more about the Lord, our faith will grow stronger, our lives will change and we will make choices that are honoring to Him. Today's verse talked about our lives being built on Him.

Are you "building your life" on His principles?

Are your relationships echoing His grace and love?

Are your business dealings reflecting His honesty and wisdom?

Is your attitude mirroring His peace?

Circumstances will always arise that try to uproot our faith, our peace, our health, and our sanity. If your faith is in Him, then you will be able to face each situation with a heart of thankfulness for all that He has done for you, in you, and all that He will do in your future, through your committed hours of spending time with Him.

Just as my family trusted my father to get us safely home in a fierce storm, you too can trust in your faith in the Lord. You can go forward into the unknown, knowing that He is with you each and every step of the way.

First published January 30, 2020 at www.ibelieve.com

Good Gifts

Gifts. We give gifts to babies when they are born. Gifts for birthdays and celebrating milestones such as losing a tooth, getting a good grade, or having a no cavity dental visit. We give Easter gifts, baptism gifts, and graduation gifts. We give gifts sometimes just for fun.

Kids get excited about their birthday or Christmas and talk about it for weeks, some even making elaborate lists of the gifts that they want. They even spend hours dreaming about the gifts that would make their life perfect. My kids usually get a few of the gifts they asked for and a few surprise ones. My kids have never been disappointed in the gifts that they have asked for or have received.

This Bible verse states that we humans are evil. We are full of sin, envy, anger and a whole lot of other attitudes that the Bible considers to be evil. Yet we still have love and generosity in our hearts toward our children.

No matter what phase my kids are going through, or their attitude in the days before a gift-giving event, it doesn't change my desire to give them a good gift. In all my years as a parent, through all of their ups and downs, I have never given them anything broken, harmful, useless or rotten. I love them and only want to give them good things.

The Bible verse says:

*"Your Father in heaven will give good gifts
to those who ask Him."*

He doesn't have any evil intent toward you. He loves you more than you can even begin to understand. He loves to give good gifts to you!

In your life right now, the good things that are happening, those are from Him.

Have you thanked Him for them?

How is your prayer life?

Are your prayers full of thanksgiving and adoration or are they just supplication?

He desires relationship with you just as much as He desires to bless you with good things.

When I take my kids to the grocery store, they never ask for me to buy them fish, broccoli or spinach. Instead, they ask for candy, ice cream and cookies. As a parent I do not give them these items because I know that it isn't good for them, it will hurt them long-term. So, I replace their sugary treats with healthier options.

Our loving Father might also be giving you what you need instead of what you asked for because He knows what is best for you. Can you trust Him to do things in His way because He truly loves you?

I love that this Bible verse uses the word Father instead of the more formal God or Lord. It shows us that God truly cares for us as His children. He hears your prayers; He knows your longings. He wants to give you good gifts. He loves you.

If my daughter asked for a new phone every year, I wouldn't give it to her. She needs to learn to wait or work for it. If she asked for a car at the age of nine, I wouldn't give it to her. She needs to wait until she is more mature. If she asked to go swimming when the pool water was freezing, I wouldn't let her. She needs to wait for her safety. My only desire is to show her love.

Perhaps we ask for things that God knows will keep us from Him, or might harm us. We can't see the whole picture of our circumstances, but God can. Perhaps God is making you wait because He loves you so much. Can you thank Him during the waiting? Can you go into today, trusting Him for the things that you cannot see?

God is lovingly working out details in your life that you cannot see. Wait for it to be unwrapped and revealed in His perfect time. It will be perfect and it will definitely be the best gift ever!

First published January 27, 2020 at www.ibelieve.com

Commit Your Way to the Lord

My husband and I were super excited to buy a house that had a pool. My oldest daughter was already an amazing swimmer and could barely wait to unpack her bathing suit and jump into her very own swimming pool! My younger daughter was two and though she loved her bath, was a bit hesitant about this whole big pool thing.

So, I hired a sweet private swim teacher to come to our pool and teach my daughter. This amazing lady was able to get my daughter to swim across to the other side of the pool all by herself, within just a few lessons.

It was wonderful that my two-year-old was able to swim and play in the pool with her sister, with me sitting on the edge.

The teacher wanted me to practice with her throughout the week, but also to have her wear arm floaties when she would get tired. Somehow, my little girl equated swimming with those arm floaties.

My two-year-old trusted her floaties to keep her safely bobbing on the surface. It gave her the freedom to enjoy every inch of the pool. She wanted to swim every day, for hours and her physical strength grew, along with her confidence. It opened up a new world for her.

She insisted on wearing them every time she got in the pool. I did allow her to wear them, but as the summer progressed, I inflated them less and less without her knowledge. It got to the point that there was absolutely no air left in them, but she still insisted on wearing them, thinking she needed them to swim.

Our walk with the Lord could be compared to my daughter using her pool floaties.

Life can be a struggle at times, and we often end up in the deep end, with the worries and concerns of our lives causing us to tread the water. Sometimes it might feel as if we can barely keep our heads above the surface. It can feel like there are too many kids jumping into the pool, their splashes making it way too difficult to see clearly.

The Bible verse tells us to:

"Commit your way to the Lord."

When my daughter decided to go swimming, she fully committed to what that meant.

She would ask me for permission, then convince her older sister to join her, and then had to go put on her bathing suit and without fail, the floaties.

She was intentional about creating this fun experience again and again all summer long.

In your schedule today, in the decisions you have to make, the people you interact with, the places you have to go, have you committed each and every one of these to the Lord?

When my little girl committed to jump into the pool, she prepared beforehand.

Perhaps if we were to be intentional about committing our day, our situations, and our relationships to the Lord, we would view our life differently. Perhaps we would experience our life in a new way.

If we were to commit our way to the Lord, we could then experience what the second part of the verse promises:

"Trust in Him and He will act."

My daughter put those floaties on each of her arms before she jumped into the deep end of the pool. She knew that no matter how many times she jumped in and went under the water, that the floaties would work. The floaties would allow her to pop back up to the surface, every single time.

If you have committed your ways today to the Lord, you can go into the day before you, trusting that He will guide, direct, and protect you.

If you have given it over to Him, then you can realize that every little thing that comes your way today, has been allowed by Him.

You can trust Him in it all. In the sickness, the successes, the smiles and tears, in sunrises and sunsets, in the new and the old.

Will you commit to the Lord the tough things in your life? You can trust in Him, knowing that He will act in every situation and for your good every single time.

So, before you move onto the next thing in your day, will you take a moment right now to commit the rest of your schedule, your decisions to Him?

Walk confidently into each situation and circumstance seeing them as opportunities to trust Him. He will act. He will not let you drown. He wants you to trust Him in everything. So put on your faith floaties, and leave your everything in His loving and capable hands.

First published December 4, 2019 at www.ibelieve.com

Dear friend,

I pray that these devotions were a blessing to you, and that they encouraged you to keep walking with Jesus.

I pray that the words I wrote caused you to examine your life to see how He is working in every single situation, teaching you His truths, and strengthening your faith.

Jeremiah 29:13 says:

"You will seek me and find me when you seek me with all your heart."

I pray that you go into each new day with a deeper hunger to seek the Lord. He promises that we *will* find Him *if* we seek Him with all our heart.

Trusting Him to complete the good work that He has begun in you,

Tiffany